The Wye Valley

Richard Sale

Photographs by Rosie Waite

Wildwood House London

First published in Great Britain in 1984
by Wildwood House Ltd
Jubilee House, Chapel Road
Hounslow, Middlesex, TW3 1TX

©1984 Richard Sale
Photographs copyright ©1984 Rosie Waite

Printed and bound in Great Britain by Camelot Press Ltd. Shirley Road, Southampton.
ISBN 0 7045 0496 0
Typeset in 10 point Plantin 1½ point leaded by TJB Photosetting Ltd. of South Witham, Lincolnshire

Contents

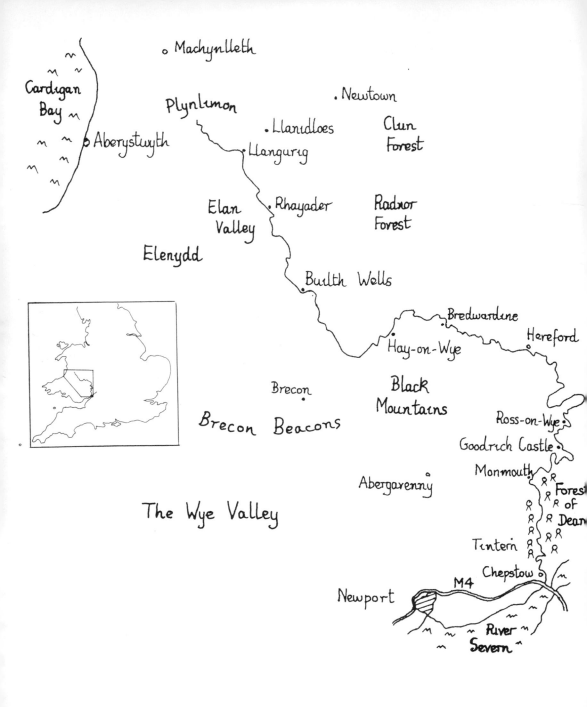

Acknowledgments

I have lived the greater part of my life within easy reach of one part or another of the Wye Valley, but not all the information in this book has been gathered first hand, or alone, and thanks are due to a number of organisations and individuals.

I am indebted to the library services of England and Wales, especially to the National Library of Wales, Aberystwyth, the county libraries of Hereford and Gloucester and Bristol Central Library.

The preparation of the book spans generations, my parents introduced me to the Valley, my son Nathan now accompanies me on journeys there. Between those two stages of my life many other people have been involved. I thank all the walkers, canoeists and rock climbers who have helped me enjoy the Valley, but especially John and Kevin Bassindale, Colin Daniels, Roger Francis, Arthur Lees, Trevor Lewis and Mike Rogers.

In addition to being grateful for services on and off water I also thank Mike Rogers for drawing the maps.

Early morning by the
Wye (Tintern)

The River Wye

I firmly believe that the River Wye flows in the finest river valley in England and Wales. I base this claim not only on the scenic beauty of the valley and the interest and architectural purity of the villages and towns that line its banks, but on its having no flaw. There is not one big ugly city near it, no factory spoiling any of its views, no process pumping opaque nastiness into its waters. Whether the visitor is looking at the mountain brook Wye with its backdrop of Welsh hills, at the slow glide of the river through the water meadows of Herefordshire, or at the meanders in the wooded lower reaches, he or she is seeing purest nature and the hand of man in moderation together.

Because of this naturalness the Valley has always attracted visitors. Perhaps the most famous visitors to the Wye Valley were those who came in the late-eighteenth and early-nineteenth centuries in search of the 'Picturesque'. This did not mean just a 'nice view', as we might say today, but a real sought-after composition. Not any view could be picturesque; it needed to have certain features, be possessed of foreground and background, of colour. The rules were actually laid down, perhaps best expressed by the Rev. Gilpin, who also did much to advertise the Wye Tour, a trip down the river, usually from Ross to

William Gilpin was born in 1724 in Cumberland, received his M.A. at Oxford and was ordained as a priest in 1752. He was at one time headmaster of Cheam and died as the vicar of a New Forest Parish in 1804. He wrote several books, but his fame lies in his *Observations on the River Wye and Several Points of South Wales* (1782), which describes his own tour of 1770, as well as the rules for the Picturesque. The book has been recently (1973) published in a facsimile reproduction. Gilpin stated his case against nature's ability to compose picturesque scenes succinctly and censoriously:

> 'Nature is always great in design. She is an admirable colourist also; and harmonizes tints with infinite variety and beauty; but she is seldom so correct in composition, as to produce an harmonious whole.'

River detail, one mile
below its source

For the Wye Gilpin noted that each view comprised the 'area', the river itself; two 'side-screens', the opposite banks; and the 'front-screen', the winding of the river. He noted that the view of the side-screens could be simple or complex, contrasting or folded. The banks could be adorned with one, or more, of four ornaments: ground, wood, rocks and buildings. The proportion of each must be right. The ground, for instance, might be broken or of the wrong colour. The trees might be in the wrong place. And so the rules go on. It really is an extraordinarily complex piece of logical breakdown of the aesthetic. The tour follows, with each view being, figuratively at least, marked out of ten. I confess to finding the idea faintly ridiculous, mildly amusing, but it did allow Gilpin to make some perceptive comments, although few would so describe his opinions on Tintern Abbey (see below).

The Wye has not only been a piece of scenery, especially to those who lived along its banks. In the time before adequate roads, and certainly before the ages of canal and railway, the river was a lifeline to the communities in Herefordshire, being the only means of transport for goods in bulk. The river was navigable to Hereford, seventy miles from the estuary, to large barges, if they were flat-bottomed. Even beyond the city there was river traffic, with a winch system at Monnington to drag the vessels past the falls. The traffic was never easy, however; in dry weather there was sometimes not enough water for the barges, and when it was wet it was sometimes impossible to move upstream against the flow of water. There were numerous plans to build weirs and locks, each producing its own arguments between merchants and fishermen, each eventually coming to nothing. Perhaps this lack of complete, and dependable, navigation caused the lack of enthusiasm for large-scale industrialism on the banks. Only in the vicinity of Tintern was there ever any real attempt to base industry near the river. The age of canals and railways and, in the case of the iron-works, competition from nearby South Wales ended this attempt, and the river returned to a more natural state.

For its use as a means of transport, for the benefit of man, the river exacted a toll of the young, the frail and the inexperienced. A man peering into the waters from a bridge once noted that it was pretty river, but that he had once known a pretty woman and she was a right bitch. The Wye, like all rivers, has a savage side, as a reading of the gravestones in churchyards that line the banks will quickly reveal. But a death is a sacrifice to the Wye; the old ladies of the villages would say, after someone had drowned, that it was now safe to allow the children to play on the banks. Until next year.

If this book were on geography, we would speak of the river in terms of youth, maturity and old age. In the case of the Wye, however, this scheme does not fit well because of rejuvenation in the lower reaches. Instead the natural changes in landscape have been used to divide the river valley into three sections: the mountain region where the river flows between high hills in Wales from Plynlimon to Hay; the plain where the river crosses the Herefordshire flat-lands from Hay to Ross; and the wooded vale below Ross where the river cuts deep into the landscape, the sides of its valley being extensively wooded.

Our exploration of the valley is total, which means that some places will be reached by road. In addition, however, three long walks are given which explore between them about half of the river's length – the Upper and Lower Wye Valley Walks, and that section of the Offa's Dyke Pathway that lies in the valley. Downstream from Glasbury the river is public, the 100 miles of river being open to anyone with a canoe and the time to use it. The canoe trip is also mentioned here. It must be stressed, however, that the book is not a true guidebook for any of the walks, although maps are given, nor does it provide a guide for the canoeist. The walker should obtain the relevant Ordnance Survey sheets (the Wye Valley is covered by sheets 135, 136, 147, 148, 149, 161 and 162). The canoeist *must* obtain a river guide.

In its journey to the sea, the Wye reaches the essence of man. In Wales it flows through country where young men carved love-spoons for their girls, the Welsh engagement ring produced from a single piece of apple wood – the apple being the tree of love. In Herefordshire it flows through villages where the sin-eater was employed to eat cakes and bread from the chest of a dead man and so consume his sins that he might go to heaven guiltless. Love and death, the essence of man.

The river sees all aspects of the history of two nations and their occasional strife. Owain Glyndwr in Plynlimon, Prince Llywelyn at Builth Wells, the castles of the Norman conquerors and of the Civil Wars, the churches and the cathedral, the ruins of an abbey. The ghosts of the past.

12

Nant-y-Moch dam

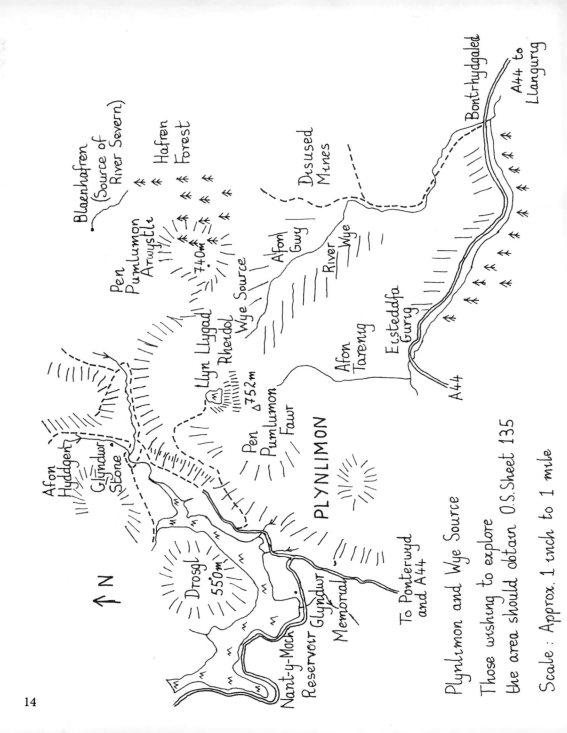

↑ N

Plynlimon and Wye Source

Those wishing to explore
the area should obtain O.S. Sheet 135

Scale : Approx. 1 inch to 1 mile

14

The Mountain (from the source to Hay-on-Wye)

Plynlimon

On a fine, cold day in late October I made my way up through the rocks of Craig Las to the east of Llyn Llygad Rheidol. I had hoped to arrive at the source of the Wye in time to take photographs, but I would not now. Already the sun was dropping rapidly to dowse itself in a flurry of red steam far out in Cardigan Bay. The Land Rover track from the shore of the tiny reservoir below Plynlimon would allow me to arrive back safely at Nant-y-Moch, so I could savour the moment of the sunset so far from 'security'. I crossed the ridge between the high Plynlimon peaks and dropped down to the south-east.

Plynlimon has a, not entirely justified, reputation for being both flat and boggy. In such country the river sources can be difficult to locate with absolute certainty and the searching may be an anticlimax. I was interested in finding the Wye source, but not overwhelmed with excitement. But the Wye does not start hesitantly among peat hags, it cuts a cleft into the hillside reaching far back towards the ridge, a deepening cleft that imposes itself on the visitor as his eye is drawn off into old Montgomeryshire. The first water can be located, there oozing out from under a clump of star-headed moss branches. Within a yard it is a trickle, several more and it is a 'nant', a brook running down to become a stream, a river. It is as though the Wye knows, even here, that it will cut a magnificent passage through its valley and must start appropriately.

I returned over the ridge impressed. The sun was almost gone now, the last of the day's light being sufficient to light a way down the steep slope to the reservoir. It was dark and cold when I reached Nant-y-Moch. It had been a good evening.

Peacock, writing in the middle of the nineteenth century, stated that

> 'the tourist who, with knowledge of its character, should hereafter attempt to ascend Plinlimmon ALONE, is little better than a fool. He has one chance of returning in safety; he has ninety-nine chances of being seen no more in life.'

Nant-y-Moch
reservoir and
Pumlumon

His assertion, though much tempered by the desire of the writers of that period to see all hills as huge and dangerous, all ravines as the clefts of hell, was based on a lone ascent when he became lost amid leg-devouring black bogland. He was fortunate, we are told, to escape from the jaws of death to tell his tale. Had he gone to the source of the Wye he would have had ninety-nine chances of enjoying his day.

That is especially true if he had started it by being awakened by the rippling call of curlews on the shore of the Nant-y-Moch reservoir, and had enjoyed a long breakfast watching the meadow pipits parachuting to earth. He would perhaps have needed a clear, windless day and, as he paused to rest, a red kite to have passed silently over him. These birds, one of the finest of British raptors, were limited to Elenydd to the south, but now can be seen searching the Plynlimon ridges for food and thermals – an elegant bird, distinctively chestnut and fork-tailed. Given all of this Peacock would have enjoyed his day. All things are relative.

Plynlimon is a strange mountain for Wales. There is none of the spiky grandeur of the Snowdonia Park peaks to the north or of the steep scarps of the Brecon Beacons Park to the south. Here, and on the high plateau of Elenydd to the immediate south, are rolling hills, gentle but high and bare. On seeing Plynlimon for the first time Jean Charlet, the guide from the Golden Age of Alpine climbing, is reputed to have been astonished: 'But God has forgotten to put tops on them.'

The name Elenydd was used to describe this mid-Wales area as long ago as the twelfth century by Giraldus (Gerald) of Wales who travelled the country with Archbishop Baldwin seeking support for the Third Crusade. It is believed to derive from the Elan river south of Plynlimon, and now famous for the reservoirs strung out along its length. But what of Plynlimon? The now a-greed Welsh form is Pumlumon, the first half derived, perhaps, from *pump* meaning five. Five what? The most usual explanation is five rivers – the Severn, the Wye, the Rheidol and two others. But why only two others since there are many? Plynlimon is the mother of rivers, and all lists differ. Perhaps then it is five peaks, five summits? Again it is difficult, Plynlimon is all high and wild, and while there are distinct summits it is not easy to see five rather than four or six.

But is that the whole story? To the north of the reservoir below Pen Pumlumon Fawr the Afon Hyddgen drains to Nant-y-Moch. Here, in this valley, in 1401, Owain Glyndwr had gathered together a small army, about 400 men, at the start of his campaign to create a Wales independent of England. The political geography of Wales at that time was not clearcut. It never really was, the Celtic tribes that made up the bulk of the population of the country having, as chief sport, tribal warfare. The Welsh had never learned to combine to defeat a common foe and any prince who looked likely to unite the country – always by violence rather than statesmanship – died of the effort, his lands immediately being divided between his sons so that the area could settle back down to internal conflict. A consequence of this was that there were in Wales many groups who were not enamoured of Glyndwr's idea of a state independent of England. One such group was the Flemish community of South Wales who were so frightened at the prospect that they raised an army, 1500 strong, and marched towards Gwynedd. By stealth they surrounded Glyndwr in the Hyddgen valley and then poured in on him. A contemporary wrote of the battle:

'They hemmed him [Glyndwr] in on all sides so that he could not possibly get off without fighting at a great disadvantage. He and his men fought manfully a great while, in their own defence, against them. Finding themselves surrounded and hard put to it, they resolved at length to make their way through or perish in the attempt; so, falling on furiously, with courage whetted with despair they put the enemy, after a sharp dispute, to confusion; and they pursued so eagerly their advantage, that they made them give ground, and in the end to fly outright, leaving 200 of their men dead on the spot of the engagement. This victory rendered Owain considerable renown and was the means to bring many to his side, that his number was greatly increased.'

Two stones are said to have been set up to commemorate the battle and two are indeed shown by the Ordnance Survey on 1:50000 sheet 135. Sheet SN78 of the 1:25000 series, and the walker, know better. A white, calcite, block stands alone, looking out of place. Is it an erratic or a memorial?

784895

Standing near it at night with a full moon above Plynlimon producing eerie shadows around the valley, it was easy to think of Glyndwr. He is an enigmatic man, saint and sinner. In death he has achieved what he could only contemplate in life, a Wales united behind him as a symbol of Welshness against the onslaught of the English. Glyndwr was a mighty man – he stood a full head above his contemporaries, wore shoulder length hair when the norm was short-back-and-sides and trained like an athlete in full armour to increase strength and stamina when most noblemen trained by hawking and wenching. He was indeed a nobleman, for though of Welsh princely stock he was brought up in the English court and acquitted himself bravely in wars against France and Scotland for his English King. At the outbreak of the rebellion, in 1400, Glyndwr was in semi-retirement, probably fifty years old and no rebel. True, there had been omens at his birth – Shakespeare lists them and offers a portrait of the rebel as a man of character – but it took the personal jealousy of a marcher

18

lord to spark the conflict. The campaign was long, fought between the English armies on the one hand and the Welsh terrain and weather, together with Glyndwr's guerilla fighters, on the other. Glyndwr promised the Welsh independence, their own laws, archbishops and universities. He gave them ravaged land, burnt cities, an economy ruined by the scorched earth policy of his followers, and subjugation to the English crown. They were worse off after the rebellion than before, and now they worship him as a symbol of our nationhood.

I walked back towards Nant-y-Moch from the Glyndwr stone, if that is what it is, passing a ruined farmhouse. The wind blowing down the Hyddgen Valley moved between the walls, and remnants of roof timber shifted creakily. A few stunted rowans are trying to grow in deep stream valleys to my left, a clump of conifers far away on the bank of the Llechwedd-mawr seems only to draw attention to the absence of trees. It was not hard to believe that the valley still holds the ghosts of the hundreds who died. And for what? Now Glyndwr is revered, but what of them? Did the crofters starving from feeding his army and then having the remaining crops slashed and burnt love him? Did the man kneeling a few yards from where I stand now, clutching his entrails in his hands, love the rebellion? Idealism is a wonderful thing at a distance. When you are dying there is only death.

A stone erected near the Nant-y-Moch dam points out that near here Owain Glyndwr raised his standard in his fight against the English. The Hill of the Standard, Pen Llumon – could *that* be the name after all, with no need to count rivers or hills?

For the morbidly curious it is said that spearheads can still be found in the Hyddgen Valley.

The images offered by the summit plateau of Plynlimon are more pleasing than those of the Hyddgen Valley. The *Mabinogion* has two of the Celtic Knights of the Round Table, Kei and Bedwyr, sit on the peak, 'in the greatest wind in the world,' and it does indeed seem to blow with more enthusiasm here than on the peaks north or south. That has to be an effect of situation rather than fact, the very openness of the landscape, the lack of shelter. The openness gives a fine panorama. Clear weather allows Snowdon itself to be seen, though usually the view is more local, taking in Cader Idris, the Arans and Arenigs to the north, Mynydd Ddu and Prescelli to the south, and inland to the Wrekin. Mention of Cader Idris prompts memory of another battle, fought in the seventh century between armies of the Merionethshire prince, Idris ap Gwyddno, and the Irish. Cader Idris *may* have been named after the victor though the battle almost certainly took place near the source of the Severn.

821899   The Severn source lies a couple of miles north-east of the source of the Wye, and is a less satisfactory place. In Welsh the river is Hafren, the source Blaenhafren, a name which has a much more satisfactory derivation than the name of our river. Geoffrey of Monmouth, of whom we shall hear again when we reach his home town, in his *History of the Kings of Britain* tells the story of Locrinus, a King of Britain who marries Gwendolen, daughter of Corineus, King of Cornwall, despite being in love with Estrildis. Eventually, when Corineus dies, Locrinus deserts Gwendolen for Estrildis and their daughter Habren or Hafren. The outraged Gwendolen flees to Cornwall, raises an army and returns to do battle with Locrinus. Locrinus is killed and Gwendolen in a fit of passion has Estrildis and Habren hurled into the river and drowned. Then, recognizing that the girl should be honoured as her husband's daughter, Gwendolen issues an edict that henceforth the river shall be called Habren. The Romans latinized the name to Sabrina, which gives us Severn. In contrast the derivation of Wye, or the Welsh form Gwy, is mundane, the only realistic suggestion being that it derives from the Welsh for cataract.

The Severn, pushed north by high ridges, achieves a longer course and at its mouth, say at the Severn Bridge, is a wide, dominating river. Some do not notice when crossing that bridge that it is preceded, or followed, by a smaller bridge over a narrow river. That is the Wye joining its bigger brother. At birth – two miles apart; at end – together.

In keeping with this physical closeness the Welsh believed there was a psychic exchange between the sources, the land between them being known as Fferllys, the abode of the Tylwyth Teg, the fair folk or fairies. The ferns here are said to bloom with a small blue flower at night on St John's Eve, especially for the Tylwyth Teg. If you are lucky enough to catch the seeds of the flowers, at midnight and in a white cloth – no hand must touch them – then you become invisible so that you may visit your lover's room. Or else stay where you are, and an elf or a rider will buy them from you with a purse full of gold. As with fairies everywhere, the Plynlimon little people were fine unless the mood took them otherwise, in which case they could be malevolent. They therefore acquired a reputation for being left alone or treated with great caution. Those who dismiss such stories as childish should bear in mind the following 'authentic' story from the turn of the century – it could stand them in good stead if they fall foul of the Plynlimon bogs. It seems that a local lost his way one night crossing the mountain and was caught in a boggy section when he came upon a number of small flickering flames – the Tylwyth Teg were dancing by the light of hand-held candles. Frightened now as much by the fear of what the folk might do to him for having interrupted their dancing, as by the bog, the man stopped. 'Ladies and gentlemen,' he called with a bow, 'would you please help a poor lost gent across the bog?' The flames immediately formed in two lines, runway lights for his crossing. At the end of the bog he turned and thanked them, wishing them a pleasant night's entertainment. The air was filled with laughter, though he only ever saw the flickering flames of the candles. Curiously enough, this tale, or one very similar, appears to have arisen (independently?) on Dartmoor, on the Cambridge fens and in other wetland areas.

When walking along the high Plynlimon plateau between the river sources it is easy to believe that the area could be home to more than just sheep. Is it the wind that is gently moaning in the valleys below? And is it a buzzard plaintively mewing, or the *bwgan*?

The Wye loses 2200 feet in height in the 135 miles from its source to the sea below Chepstow. Of these 2200 feet it loses half by the time it reaches Bontrhydgaled, its first bridge. A footpath follows the river down the last two miles of its four-mile journey from source to bridge, following the track used by miners who dug lead from the sides of Plynlimon. It is an ironic thought that the Wye, now one of Britain's most unspoilt rivers, should at one stage, just a little over 100 years ago, have been scorned as lead-polluted.

To the west from here, just beyond Ponterwyd, the visitor can walk into the hillside at the Llywernog mining museum. It is an interesting site using waterwheels, which the modern ecologist thinks everyone should install and the old miners could not wait to replace with steam power. The reasons for both opinions are obvious – water power is free, but a forty-foot diameter wheel producing twentyfive horse power would lower the water level in a ten acre pond by two-and-a-half feet every day.

Until the coming of industrialization on a vast scale Wales was an important country, with metal ore deposits in all counties. Those who wish to visit an ancient site should go to Cwmystwyth, the valley immediately south of the Wye. There the standard, wind-swept site with ruined buildings and spoil heaps is very atmospheric.

At Bontrhydgaled the Wye is joined by the Tarenig, a larger, more impressive stream that has risen on the southern flank of Pen Pumlumon Fawr not a mile from the Wye. It is the Wye that changes direction at the confluence. The Tarenig has also flowed further, but our stream has the distinction of having risen something over 100 feet further up the mountain. The Tarenig has flowed through Eisteddfa Gurig, the first named hamlet on water that will be the Wye water. St Curig was a sixth-century saint who landed in Wales at Aberystwyth (from Ireland?) and made his way inland. Here at Eisteddfa Gurig the saint rested. If it was his first rest since Aberystwyth, then he was no mean walker, but clearly this lonely, windswept spot did not suit him and he followed the Tarenig/Wye Valley down to Llangurig, where he established his first church. Those not familiar with the Welsh language will have noticed the difference in

The Wye, two miles
below its source near
Bontrhydgaled

Conifers at
Bontrhydgaled

spelling between St Curig and Llangurig – the *clas* (or monastic house) of Curig. In addition to the obvious difficulties of Welsh – the use of *dd, ff* and *ll* as separate letters, the use of *w* as a vowel, the pronunciation of *f* as *v* – there is also the mutation, the changing of the first letter of a word on occasions, depending upon what precedes it. The change is to make the second word sound more pleasing, but does little for the novice.

Those familiar with the journey of George Borrow will also know that the local guide he hired for his walk in this area thought that Eisteddfa was named from the resting point of three wise men from different parts of the world who sat here and told each other histories. What the histories were of eluded the man, except that he believed the Tylwyth Teg were included, but it does suggest that the locals were not entirely aware, or did not accept, the story of St Curig in the mid-nineteenth century.

Between Bontrhydgaled and Llangurig there is a very fine piece of high mountain valley. The view up the valley could be improved if the apparently endless regiments of spruce on the southern side were broken up with some broad-leaves. Usually the only relief, and that poor, is a scarred section of hillside where the trees have been cut away. But the northern valley side is true mountain with its slate outcrops and yellow gorse.

Below the conifers on the southern side, footpaths, neither well signed nor distinct, follow the river as the valley widens towards Llangurig. Here we are 1500 feet down from the summit of Plynlimon and the trees are no longer stunted, the last mile into the village being through an avenue of broad leaves.

Llangurig

Llangurig is the first village reached on our journey to the sea, and it is worth a stop. It was here that Curig Lwyd or Curig Farchog – Curig the Blessed or the Knight, as St Curig was then known – stopped on his journey into Wales. Curig was a sixth-century monk with an eye for a restful spot, for it was here that he decided to build a 'clas.' A *clas* was one of the earlier forms of monastic house, a church with a group of huts for the monks and a small graveyard. The Welsh word *llan* refers to the same sort of hamlet, the *clas* being the 'mother-house', where the founding monk or a later abbot lived, the *llan* being a daughter-house. Invariably the sites were set close to water, and in a valley to offer some shelter to the monks, whose life was austere. When Curig landed in mid-Wales the land was controlled by Maelgwn Gwynedd, known as the Dragon, a man of huge physical stature and an equally huge capacity for violence. He was obviously impressed with Curig's bearing, for he gave him land here to found his *clas*.

Just south of
Llangurig

Perhaps there was a distant understanding between the men, for Curig was a converted warrior, and Maelgwn was in need of salvation.

We do not know if Curig managed to persuade Maelgwn to a more Christian approach to his political problems, although the saint may have been present during the king's final hours. Maelgwn died in 547, while Curig died on 17 February 550. The fact that the date is known so accurately is indicative of the awe in which the man was held.

It is probable that following the saint's death the *clas* continued, perhaps a *llan* by then, although it is unlikely that it survived, except in a very basic form, the coming of the Normans to Britain. The Normans never invaded Wales in any realistic sense, that not, apparently, being part of William's grand plan. Instead he set up, on the border, or march, of England and Wales, the marcher lords, whose western boundary to their estates was of their own choosing. Encroachments were made and resisted for many years. The Normans also brought to Britain their own monastic tradition, and an abbey was built at Strata Florida, south of Llangurig, within a century of the conquest. Very quickly the abbey's area of influence, and possession, had expanded to include Llangurig.

Now the church has little that dates even from the fourteenth century. It is a quiet site, the building set in its circular churchyard, and has some aspects that are of interest, despite having been vandalized in the early nineteenth century by restorers intent on 'improving' it. Much of the restoration work was paid for by J.Y.W. Lloyd of Clochfaen, an excellent house about half a mile south of the village. Lloyd was the curate of Llandinam, north-east beyond Llanidloes, who converted to Catholicism, joined the Papal Zouaves – the Vatican Foreign Legion, for want of a better description – and was knighted by the Pope. Chevalier Lloyd then rejoined the Church of England and contributed around £11,000 – a great deal of money in the latter part of the nineteenth century – to the changes in the church.

As though to respond to all this piety, nature offered, in the last quarter of the nineteenth century, a Christmas thorn. Its existence was confirmed by the Rev. Francis Kilvert, of whom we shall speak again as the river enters England, who came on Christmas Eve in 1875 to see the tree growing in the crags above the river at Dolfach farm, a couple of miles south of the village. Kilvert found fifteen people gathered around the tree at midnight all entranced, awaiting the miracle. Later an old man took a cutting of the tree to Bredwardine for Kilvert, and grafted it onto a hawthorn there. The graft took and the tree blossomed on a cruelly cold Christmas Day. Within the year Kilvert was dead.

Not all the magic practised at Llangurig was white, however, for the village was well known as the home of conjurors, necromancers and witches. The Evil Eye was available to those who lived in one house; it survived three generations in the building, and was so powerful that it could cause horses to lose the use of their limbs. This particular form of sorcery was performed by both men and women, being 'witchcraft' only when the practitioner was a (usually old, ugly and disliked) woman. The local conjurors were often needed to sort out the magic, as they were in touch with the Tylwyth Teg. One such conjuror explained to a hunter that he needed a sixpence, not shot, in his gun to shoot a particularly fine hare that had been seen often around the village. The puzzled hunter did this and at last hit the hare in the leg. He followed it as it limped into a thicket. Beyond the thicket was a cottage and in it an old and ugly woman who had just, she said, fallen and broken her leg. Such stories of witches transforming themselves into animals are not, of course, peculiar to Llangurig but they do seem to abound in this area.

Indeed the village seems steeped in tales from the darker side of folk legend or memory. Here we are at the centre of an area in which the *canwyll corph*, or corpse candle, was a harbinger of death. The candles could be seen, single flickering lights, moving across the countryside, heading towards the house of some poor individual who was to die. Nor were they disembodied lights, the candle itself being very real. One man returning from a market to Llangurig late one night was shielding his head from the wind and rain and so did not see a *canwyll corph*. The candle was not for him, but it hit him on the head as it flew along, killing him instantly. Since the candle had no conscience, it continued its journey, foretelling the death of an old woman who died soon after.

Such stories are dismissible as fantasies, but the custom, known as Arian-y-rhaw, of the parish clerk to hold a shovel over the grave at a funeral for the mourners to drop a silver coin onto was very real. The vicars of the church were, not surprisingly, unhappy with such rites as they were almost certainly rooted in paganism, but some villagers showed the correct amount of disdain. One funeral was attended by a man who had walked five miles, arriving with only a silver sixpence and a considerable thirst. He cunningly changed his sixpence into six old pennies, which he dropped onto the clerk's shovel. The clerk, who also happened to be landlord of the village's Upper Inn, refused the copper coins in horror. The man replied: 'I am obliged to you; our friend Evan Davies [the landlord of the Lower Inn] will gladly receive them.'

The churchyard where this story originated is left by going through a lych gate of the mid-nineteenth century opposite which is a more prosaic spot, a quaint stone fountain complete with slate tiled roof. The inscription on the fountain records that the first water supply was given to the village in 1888 by Col. George Hope Lloyd Berney. Elsewhere the village is pleasant without being awe-inspiring. There is the ubiquitous craft shop, and opposite a fine old chapel four-square against weather and conformity.

Two miles north of
Rhayader

Below Llangurig the Wye Valley is, when the time is right, very green. That we are still in upland Wales is evident from the high ridge of Elenydd that separates the southern bank of the Wye from the valley of the Elan. This is fine country, with a scattering of small farmhouses and the white dots of sheep on the high grass ridges. The traveller who wishes to see the river section from Llangurig to Rhayader at its best should give the A470 a rest and take the lane that follows the right bank. At first the valley is wide and flat-bottomed, with little tree cover, but it becomes narrower as the confluence with the Marteg is approached. Here, as our river and road swing sharply south, there is a beautiful section, the immediate river banks heavily forested with broad leaves and with fine outcrops on the Elenydd escarpment adding a rugged touch. The Afon Marteg flows down a steep, bare valley, along which the traveller would soon reach the village of St Harmon. This was the site of another *clas*, founded by St Germanus, or St Garmon as he was also known. It is of interest because the church here possessed the staff of St Curig, although why it was not at Llangurig is not clear. Giraldus saw the staff, describing it as encased in gold and silver with the top a roughly shaped cross. It was, of course, a miraculous relic, Giraldus maintaining that it was particularly effective in smoothing away the pus from glandular swellings and tumours. Very nice.

As was usual, the staff did not work for nothing, the going rate being one penny per swelling, payable to the vicar. Once, says Giraldus, a person handed over a halfpenny, and only half his swelling went down. He offered the other halfpenny and was cured. Another man was granted credit because of poverty and was cured but did not pay by the agreed date. His swelling immediately returned and only when he had paid threepence (a very high rate of interest!) was he returned to health. At the time of the Dissolution of the Monasteries such a relic would have been confiscated, as were many phials of Sacred Blood and splinters of the True Cross, particularly as it was of gold. What exactly happened is unclear. One story says it was burnt, which is possible if it was first stripped or if the gold was of little value. Another story maintains that it was hidden away, and as those responsible for this were soon dead, it lies buried still.

The view up the Nant y Sarn valley from below the Marteg confluence is excellent. Across the headwall of this valley a pathway links our river with Pont ar Elan where the Elan joins the Craig Goch reservoir. This excellent walk is marked on the First Series OS 1:50000 sheet 147 as an Ancient Road. By the time they had produced the Landranger series this description was omitted. Whether it was or not, this is a fine walk when the weather allows.

Beyond the Marteg confluence the Wye Valley becomes very narrow and tree-lined. In this section there are several suspension bridges linking the fields of farms split by the river. They seem, at first sight, incongruous, but do lend a little unexpected romance to the valley.

Suspension bridge
between Llangurig
and Rhayader

The Wye at
Rhayader

Rhayader

Rhayader is the first of many fortified towns that we meet as we travel down river, though almost nothing of its castle now remains. It is named, so it is believed, from Rhaedr Gwy, the waterfall on the Wye, though the stream that flows into the Wye just south of the town is called the Rhyd-hir.

The castle was not, in fact, Norman, but built by a Welsh prince, Rhys ap Grufydd, to defend his land against incursions by the Norman marcher lords. It was a fine building, strongly constructed. We hear that in 1178, soon after its construction, it was besieged by northern enemies of Rhys but 'after having lain before it a considerable time they raised the siege and returned to their own country disappointed.' After that Rhys had reasons to rue its existence when he was imprisoned there by his own sons, and in 1194 it was destroyed by fire in a battle between the family factions. The theme of siege and fire was repeated several times. On one occasion the fire was not limited to the castle. It seems that the church at Glascwm, to the east of Builth Wells, had a handbell imbued with miraculous powers because it had belonged to St David. Anxious that her husband should be freed from Rhayader Castle a woman took the bell to the castle. There the keepers refused to free the man, and stole the bell, hanging it on a convenient wall. That night the town and castle were razed by fire, the only wall remaining intact being that on which the bell hung. There is no record of what happened to the prisoner, but since he was chained up in the castle we should fear the worst.

Finally, in 1231, Llywelyn attacked the castle, then held by the marcher lord Mortimer. The castle was fired and then smashed, the garrison killed. Later, at the time of the Civil War, what little remained was destroyed completely. During excavation work at St Clement's church, a row of regularly spaced skeletons was discovered with one very large skeleton led in the opposite direction to all the rest. Could these have been the garrison and its commander?

Today the town is just an ordinary mid-Wales market town, a centre for pony trekkers and tourists visiting the Elan Valley. Its market, for sheep and cattle, is on Wednesday, and there is a pony sale every Autumn. It is a quiet spot, the clock tower in the centre being a focal point, but the streets to the south-west leading down to the river are worthwhile to follow.

Periodically the quiet has been shattered. Before the castle brought its misery Vortigern came here, seeking a refuge from the pursuing horde of Saxons under Hengist. Vortigern was the British king who, during a time of civil war in Britain, called for help from the Saxons and was rewarded with an army that refused to go home and eventually turned on him. After the blood and fire of the castle period Rhayader took a part in the story of the Plant de Bat, the children of Bat. In a generally lawless period in the seventeenth century these 'children', two youths and their sister, terrorized the neighbourhood, robbing travellers and stealing from farms and houses. They lived, or at least had a hide-out, in caves at the foot of the Mynach Falls at what is now called Devil's Bridge. One day they robbed a gentleman who fought back vigorously and was killed. The gentleman was no ordinary traveller, however, and his rich and powerful friends got together a small army of men who sought the Bats. They caught them at their cave, which they destroyed so that it could never again be used, and brought them to Rhayader. There they were tried and convicted. The two boys were hanged, their sister being burnt at the stake.

About two miles to the north-west of the town on the ridge top between the Wye and the Elan is Maen Serth, a standing stone. Stones like this one, which stands about seven feet tall, are usually attributed to the Neolithic or Bronze Ages, but this one has been incised with a cross. It is not known if this was added to the stone as a memorial or whether the stone is really a grave marker. A legend relates that a judge on his way to the Rhayader Assizes was robbed and murdered here. Perhaps he was the important gentleman victim of the Plant de Bat?

Since death is our theme it is worth mentioning that here at Rhayader, as at Llangurig, there was a strange funeral custom, one that continued into the twentieth century. As a funeral procession made its way to the church the mourners would, at a certain spot, throw a stone onto a cairn created by many such stones. At the same time they would say 'Carn ar dy ben', A stone on thy head. No convincing origin has been claimed for this custom; it is not even clear whether it is pagan or Celtic in origin.

As light relief from death and funeral customs we could talk of men dressed as women. In Rhayader, though, even that was not funny, for it was the scene of some of the worst of the Welsh Rebecca riots. These were against the turnpike roads, set up under an Act of Parliament to improve the road systems. In theory the idea was sound, but in practice it was iniquitous, with locals being made to pay tolls on roads that were not kept in good repair, while the turnpike owners just pocketed the fees, and occasionally having to pay for the repairs as well through local taxes. In protest the locals dressed as women, taking their cue from Rebecca and the Old Testament that they should rise up and possess the gates of their oppressors. Usually gangs of 100, sometimes 400, men would attack and destroy a turnpike gate.

At Rhayader the visitor can join the Upper Wye Valley Walk. This walk is less well known than that which follows the final part of the valley to Chepstow, but is very worthwhile. It has been prepared by Powys County Council, who have produced four leaflets on it, showing the route, which is thirtyfive miles long,

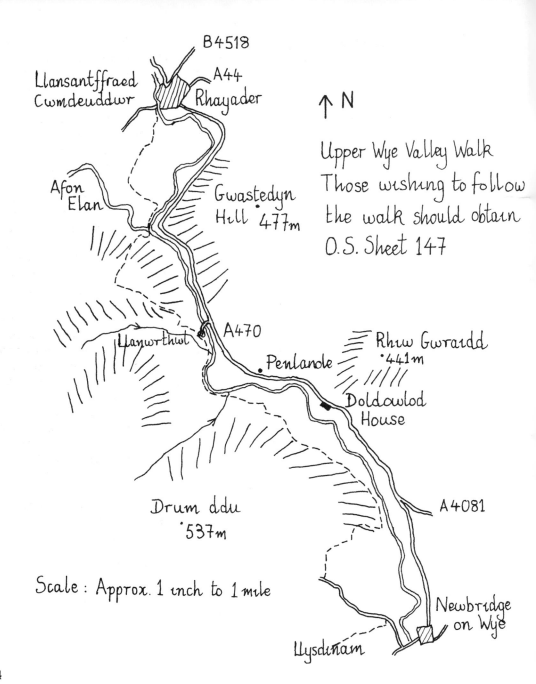

B4518

Llansantffraed
Cwmdeuddwr

A44
Rhayader

↑ N

Upper Wye Valley Walk
Those wishing to follow
the walk should obtain
O.S. Sheet 147

Afon
Elan

Gwastedyn
Hill ·477m

Llanwrthwl

A470

Penlanole

Rhiw Gwraidd
·441m

Doldowlod
House

Drum ddu
·537m

A4081

Scale: Approx. 1 inch to 1 mile

Newbridge
on Wye

Llysdinam

from Rhayader to Hay-on-Wye. Neither the leaflets nor the maps given in this book are intended to be definitive and walkers are strongly advised to obtain Ordnance Survey sheets 147, 148 and 161. The signposting and waymarking of the route varies from the ordinary to the non-existent, and anyone getting off line and not having his own maps could become badly lost. In the upper valley there are not always public footpaths along the river bank, and the route occasionally leaves the river for short sections. Some of these involve climbing hills, but nowhere is the climbing strenuous. In general any walker with a little experience of country walking and a knowledge of map reading will find the route straightforward.

The walk starts in excellent style crossing the Wye bridge and passing the church in Llansantffraed-Cwmdeuddwr. What a superb name! It is at times like this that the visitor has sympathy with Nathaniel Hawthorne, the nineteenth-century American writer who visited Bangor and there hired a coach and two horses for 'some Welsh place, the name of which I forget; neither can I remember a single name of any of the places through which we posted on that day, nor could I spell them if I heard them pronounced, nor pronounce them if I saw them spelt.'

The Wye Walk now goes past Glan Elan and follows excellent green lanes alongside a disused railway and down to the suspension bridge over the Elan river near its confluence with the Wye. If disused railways do not sound too exciting it should be remembered that such sites represent one of the few truly wild environments now to be found in Britain and are excellent for both flora and fauna.

At the Elan/Wye confluence we are at one of the better points for salmon fishing on the river; at least that was the case before over-fishing denuded the river somewhat. Around Rhayader there was good poaching as well as fishing, stories of the former being rife. It was said that two brothers lived hereabouts, one of whom was a poacher, the other a preacher. One Sunday the poacher was caught but gave his brother's name and shaved off his beard at home. When his brother was summonsed he took his congregation to court to provide an alibi and so confused the magistrate that the case was dismissed. It was maintained that the magistrate was still wondering how the preacher had managed it many years later.

It is difficult to defend lawlessness, but it has to be remembered that to the poacher the real crime was that there existed a gentleman of leisure with nothing better to do than make it hard to catch fish, while the poacher, who worked all day for little money, was only trying to feed his family.

Llansantffraed-
Cwmdeuddwr church

The River Elan joins the Wye after flowing through one of the wildest and most distinctive of all Welsh valleys. The river rises on the high land of Elenydd, a barren, almost featureless plateau that offers the wilderness-seeker one of his last opportunities in Wales. The Valley is distinctive because of its reservoirs. There are four, Caban Coch, Garreg Ddu, Pen-y-garreg and Craig Goch, on the Elan and a fifth on the Claerwen that joins the Elan in the Caban Coch reservoir. The water in the reservoirs is supplied to Birmingham, a fact that has caused a great deal of acrimony at numerous times since the first work was opened by King Edward VII in 1904. When the reservoirs were filled, eighteen houses were submerged, together with a school and church. One of the farmhouses that stood in the path of the rising water of the Claerwen, which was not opened until 1952, was dismantled and reassembled at the Welsh Folk Museum at St Fagans near Cardiff. An interesting sidelight on the destruction of the valleys was that the engineers' plan to encase the graves of the church was squashed by the locals, who did not want their ancestors to have to fight their way through several feet of concrete in order to answer the last trump. Instead the bodies were exhumed and taken to another (more?) final resting place. The dams of the two valleys now hold back 22,000 million gallons of water. The system is a considerable engineering feat regardless of the rights or wrongs of its creation and shows the impact that man can have on the environment. Some water that fell as rain on Elenydd, destined to flow in the Elan and the Wye to the Bristol Channel, is now piped to Birmingham to flow even further east and to finish in the North Sea.

The Valley is famous for the small part it played in the life of the poet Shelley, although it is often wrongly stated that he lived at Nantgwyllt, one of the mansions flooded by the reservoirs. In fact the poet was related to the Groves family who owned Cwm Elan, another mansion that was flooded, and stayed there after his expulsion from Oxford in 1811. When, in 1812, he eloped with Harriet Westbrook, the daughter of a London coffee-house keeper, it was to the Elan Valley that they came after their Scottish wedding. He then tried, but in vain, to buy Nantgwyllt. It is to be hoped that the pair were happy here, for their happiness was transitory. They broke up in 1814, Harriet drowning herself in the Serpentine in 1816 and Shelley drowning in the Mediterranean in 1822.

He was remembered in the area as an odd young man. He once sailed a boat in the Elan with a cat as crew and a £5 note as sail! A strange young man playing with water in front of a house that was to be drowned after he himself had drowned. . . .

It would be exciting to return now to the time when the Valley was as it was, or to when the waters were rising. But enough is enough now, and it is to be hoped that the proposal to increase the reservoir hold by 250% will be abandoned finally.

The Wye between
Rhayader and
Newbridge

Beyond the suspension bridge that crosses the Elan, the Wye Walk climbs the ridge on the southern (now strictly speaking the western) bank of the river. From the summit there are excellent views back towards Rhayader. Indeed the whole of the route that the walker has followed, such as it is at present, can be seen in the greatest detail. Also seen to good effect is Gwastedyn Hill, forming the other side of the valley at this point. The hill has been a haven in the past for those looking for a suitable spot for stone immortality. Its summit boasts a number of ancient cairns, a stone circle, the site of a find of Roman jewellery, and a pillar erected to celebrate the Silver Jubilee of 1977. From our vantage point something of these stone structures is visible, but the scene is dominated by the quarry at the base of the hill. Neither is this, as with the Plynlimon lead mines, the ghost of past deeds, as the gentle boom of explosives will assure you if you are present at the right time. The quarry produces a very hard stone, greywacke, much prized by road builders. One of the great joys of the Wye is the absence, along virtually the whole of its 135-mile course, of substantial industry. It is a strange fact that this quarry, in the heart of rural Wales, is the closest to such a site we will ever be. And even it does not call on the waters of the Wye to assist its process and so leave them muddier than before.

Beyond the summit of the ridge the Wye Walk drops down, with an expanding view south-west, to the village of Llanwrthwl. The village is tiny and possesses neither shops nor pub, just a few houses close to its *llan*, here dedicated to St Gwrthwl. From the A470 the village is reached across a very modern bridge that offers good views of the river both upstream and downstream. The valley is still mountain-defined here, but is becoming greener, the greens now having a greater variety.

Less than a mile downstream of the bridge is, on the left, Penlanole, a house of the mid-nineteenth century. It was built by a tea planter on his retirement from India. I am no expert so cannot judge, but an expert has said that it is so colonial in appearance that 'if the Wye . . . could . . . be converted into the Ganges, the illusion would be complete.' To stay with history and architecture, Doldowlod House, another mile downstream, is a mock-Elizabethan mansion built in the latter part of the nineteenth century by James Watt, the son of the inventor of the steam engine. It started life as a farmhouse, bought by Watt senior when he fell in love with its position during a visit to Radnorshire. The Watts actually bought a total of 10,000 acres around the house, the eviction of sitting tenants on some of the properties causing considerable local ill-feeling. Ancestors of Watt still live in the house, which is not open to the public.

Those on the Wye Walk will see the house, set off beautifully against the wooded hill of Rhiw Gwraidd, as they contour around the valley side towards Newbridge. Soon, however, the river itself has to be left, for although an old railway heads straight off into Newbridge, the way heads westward and upward to pick up tracks and minor roads into the village. It would seem to be advantageous if the way stayed close to the river at all times, but it must be remembered that it can only follow existing Rights of Way, and the occasional excursion up the valley side does offer better views.

010588 The Wye Walk does not actually visit Newbridge but turns right beforehand. A little over half a mile brings the wayfarer to the village, however, and it is worth the effort. Newbridge is a straggling place, set on the main road up and down the hill, but it has a fine church built in only twelve months and virtually a mausoleum to the Venables family who raised it. The church was built in 1882, replacing one which Kilvert called 'the beautiful little iron church'. With its displaced tower/spire and pentagon sanctuary, it is well worth a visit. Within the confines of the parish are bridges over both the Wye and the Ithon, a large tributary that joins the river a couple of miles south. For one or other of these the village is named. To hazard a guess as to which is fraught with danger as there have been numerous floodings here that have removed one or other or both bridges. One memorable flood was in early 1795, when almost all the bridges on the Wye and its tributaries from here to the Herefordshire border were swept away during a two-month period.

Those particularly interested in church architecture will probably find the trip to Disserth, a mile or so east of Newbridge, worthwhile. The church there, dedicated to St Cewydd, with its squat castellated tower sits in an excellent position close to the Afon Ithon. The tower contains the oldest church bell in old Radnorshire, dating from around 1300. The church's internal work is particularly fine; note especially the rare box pews each marked with the name of its owner. Kilvert records a story of the Rev. Thomas, Vicar of Disserth, an eccentric who would arrive in the pulpit with no sermon prepared, congratulate the congregation for turning up and for the fine day they had brought with them, and then launch into some ad lib text. Kilvert's example is exquisite, Thomas offering Mr Noah as text and starting: 'Mr Noah, he did go on with the ark, thump, thump, thump.' Wicked fellows then arrived on the scene. 'Now Mr Noah, don't go on there, thump, thump, thump, come and have a pint of ale at the Red Lion. There is capital ale at the Red Lion, Mr Noah.' By way of explanation, it not necessarily being obvious to the congregation that there were pubs in Old Testament Israel, Mr Thomas would suggest that just like us, here and now, Mr Noah had a Red Lion close to the ark, just round the corner in fact. Such preachers could increase congregations today.

Another unusual Vicar of Disserth appears in history after many of the locals had been frightened by the ghost of a farmer. It seems that the ghost had the unpopular habit of appearing behind people who were on the road from Disserth to Builth, apparently for the express purpose of frightening them witless. The ghost was highly successful, so good in fact that it became necessary to dispose of it. The Disserth vicar therefore decided to exorcise the graveyard. For a long time he wrestled alone in the church with the spirit, finally emerging triumphant having forced it into a bluebottle. The amazed locals were delighted, the bluebottle presumably less so. To complete the task, the vicar put the fly in an empty snuff box and buried it deep in a local bog, explaining that burials in wet ground laid spirits for all time, whereas those in dry ground allowed the spirit to rise again after one hundred years.

010588   When the Wye Walk turns right, instead of left into Newbridge, it passes Llysdinam Hall almost immediately. The hall stood, in the days before the whole area became Powys, in Breconshire, the Wye having formed the old county boundary. The hall, like Doldowlod, was originally a farmhouse, extended and improved in this case by Richard Venables, Archdeacon of Carmarthen, who held many civil positions in Radnorshire. His son, also Richard, was at one stage vicar of Clyro, passing into history as Francis Kilvert's rector. Kilvert paints as good a picture as any of the views obtainable from this section of the Wye Valley when he describes a February walk that he made with Venables to the summit of Drum ddu to the north-west of the hall. From the peak they could see both Plynlimon and Cader Idris, snow covered, to the north-west and the 'horns' of Carmarthen and Brecon on Mynydd Ddu – also, but less correctly, known as the Carmarthen Van or Black Mountain – to the south-west. Mr Venables, we read, slipped and fell heavily head over heels, 'but he saved his opera glasses'!

From Llysdinam the Wye Walk moves steadily westward, before turning south to pick up a minor road and then pathways that are followed all the way to Builth Wells. This section, at least in the early stages, is quite far from the river, although it is, strictly speaking, still in the valley, or on its confining ridge.

984566   Soon the 'barn' church of Llanfihangel Brynpabaum is passed. This could contain work from as early as the thirteenth century and has a fascinating stoup for holding holy water with a strange carved-head corbel above it. To the south-west from here, at Llanafon Fawr, is a church that saw another of Giraldus's miraculous events, of which he was a great collector. Here, in the reign of Henry I, a man spent the night in church with his dogs. Why he should have wanted to do so is not explained, but when found the following morning the dogs were mad and the man blind, retribution for the great irreverence. As a penance the man had himself led to Jerusalem at the time of a Crusade. When he reached the city he was tied on to a warhorse and charged into battle. Not surprisingly he was killed almost instantly. Giraldus saw this as the man ending his life with honour.

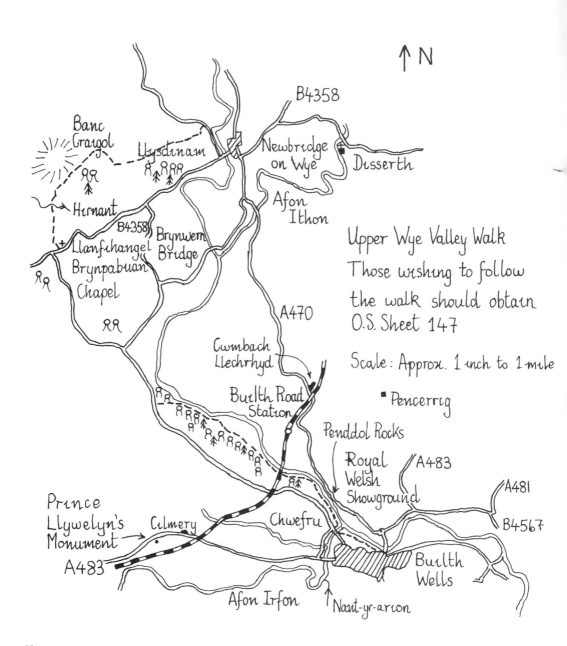

↑ N

B4358

Banc
Graigol
Llysdinam
Newbridge
on Wye
Disserth

Hirnant

Afon
Ithon

B4358
Brynwern
Bridge

Llanfihangel
Brynpabuan
Chapel

A470

Upper Wye Valley Walk
Those wishing to follow
the walk should obtain
O.S. Sheet 147

Cwmbach
Llechrhyd

Scale: Approx. 1 inch to 1 mile

Builth Road
Station

■ Pencerrig

Penddol Rocks

Royal
Welsh
Showground

A483

A481

B4567

Prince
Llywelyn's
Monument
Cilmery
Chwefru

Builth
Wells

A483

Afon Irfon
Nant-yr-arion

Oak, Cwmbach

032521   The Penddol Rocks in the Wye itself are picturesque, particularly when the river is carrying enough water for it to seethe over them. At this point the river banks are also less well defined, with rush beds that attract an interesting variety of bird life.

    Those exploring by car can take the minor road that leads off right from the 017575   A470 just south of Newbridge which soon crosses a new Brynwern bridge. The parapets of the old bridge remain, with signs giving its completion date and the names of those responsible for its design and construction. It is a good memorial to them, the older structure having more character than the newer, functional bridge. Here the road explorer soon meets the wayfarer, as the Wye Walk follows this road towards Builth Wells. The A470 passes many fine rhododendron bushes and then goes through one more village before reaching the town, that of Llechrhyd, or Cwmbach as the Ordnance Survey has it. The latter makes it sound as though the village is imploring the visitor to return. A little to the east of the village is Pencerrig, a house set in an estate famous for its oak trees. It was from these that the keel of the *Royal George*, that 'paragon of beauty,' the 'ultimate of perfection' of marine architecture, which sank in 1782 near Spithead, was constructed.

Builth Wells

In Welsh the town is Llanfair-ym-Muallt, the church of St Mary in Builth. The latter name is very ancient, probably deriving from *bu gwellt*, meaning a cow pasture. Then as now the land beside the Wye was excellent grassland. The English form takes over Builth from the ancient name, Wells having been added only recently when the town achieved a transitory fame as a spa. The more famous spa, Llandrindod, also has the name addition, though Newbridge, which we have just left, never did, its position as a spa town (or spa village) having been more tenuous.

The town site is a very ancient one, having yielded Roman relics and, it is known, having had a settlement that was razed by the Danes in 893. It is for the castle and the part it played in the final hours of the last Welsh prince that the town is most famous, an ironic situation since all that remains of the castle now is a green mound above the A470 on the eastern edge of the town. The first castle was built in the late eleventh century by Philip de Breos, a Norman marcher lord, to defend the land he had taken from the local Welsh prince. A descendant of Philip, Reginald, eventually lost the castle to the Welsh in a story as strange as most stories in Welsh history. Reginald was married to Llywelyn the Great's (Llywelyn ap Iorwerth) daughter Gwladys, and the two fought against King John, who was Llywelyn's father-in-law, the Welshman's wife Joan being an illegitimate daughter of the king. Later Reginald supported Henry III and earned Llywelyn's dislike. This dislike was fuelled by the fact that Reginald's son William had an affair with Joan while a captive of Llywelyn's. Since one of the prices William paid for his freedom – the other was a ransom of 3,000 marks – was agreement for his daughter Isabel to marry Llywelyn's son Dafydd, this implies that William was having an affair with his grandmother while his daughter (her great-granddaughter) was engaged to his uncle! Can this be right? The outcome was clear enough, if the incestuous relationships are murky. William was hanged by Llywelyn, who also captured and destroyed Builth castle.

In 1277 Edward I gave orders for a second castle to be built, part of the great ring of stone to enclose the Welsh. In the five years that followed, the 'most perfect castle ever built' was constructed, probably under the guidance of James of St George, as its concentric design was a first try for his masterpieces on the north coast. It was completed, in 1282, in time to enter Welsh history as the scene of great infamy. In that year Llywelyn the Last (Llywelyn ap Gruffydd), who was continuing the Welsh struggle against Edward I from his stronghold in the Gwynedd mountains, was lured from those mountains by the story that John Giffard, governor of the newly completed Builth castle, was willing to

December morning,
near Builth Wells

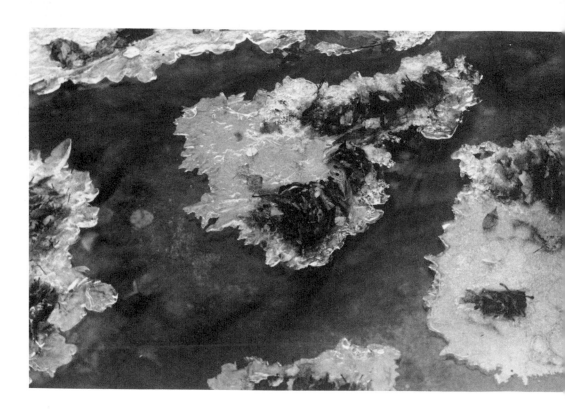

surrender the castle to him. Since Giffard had fought with Llywelyn against Henry III before changing sides, Llywelyn believed the story and rode to the area with a small group of men. It is likely that the band was only twenty strong, Llywelyn presumably not wanting to attract attention.

Llywelyn, 'the dark eagle of the north, the chief of the golden bordered shield', and his men arrived in the Builth area with the ground snow-covered and the Wye running high on melt water. He forded the river at Llechrydd Cwmbach, leaving men to hold the ford, and continued to Aberedw. There he waited, in a cave named for him to this day, but no message of invitation came, only word that the English were moving into the area to surround him. Realizing he was betrayed, Llywelyn had the local blacksmith shoe his horses backwards so that their tracks in the snow would confuse the English. He then rode back to Cwmbach, but found the river impassably high. Presumably Llywelyn was now either concerned to reach the safety of the western bank of the Wye, or still thought he could gain the safety of Builth castle. Whatever is the truth, he took his men to Builth bridge, which he either held, leaving men there, or destroyed. It is all a little confusing since open warfare on a bridge defeats the stealth of the reversed horseshoes. The trick of the horseshoes, if they were ever employed, was discovered when the blacksmith told the English, perhaps on pain of being held over his own coals, and the Welsh were surprised at the bridge. They held out, however, until another English band, who had forded the river at Erwood to the south, came on them from behind, when they were all killed. The English then split up to look for the prince. One band of men met two Welshmen a couple of miles to the west of the bridge, near to the Irfon river. Adam Francton, an English soldier, caught one Welshman as he came out of a barn and ran a spear into his side. The English then rode on. Later Francton came back, though why is not clear, to discover that the Welshman he had speared had died of his wounds. The man was being attended by a monk, who had absolved him as he lay dying, and then recognized him as Llywelyn. Francton was delighted. He cut off the prince's head and washed it in a stream before carrying it off to Builth. The head was taken to the King at Rhuddlan and then exhibited in London, crowned with ivy. There, at the Tower, the head was allowed to rot away. Llywelyn's headless body was, reputedly, taken to Abbey Cwmhir for burial.

Around the death the usual legends arose. It was said that Llywelyn was caught in a field of broom, that as he lay dying he cursed the plant for not hiding him, and that from then on no broom will grow near the spot. It was also said that the spring where the head was washed ran red for a whole day.

With the death of Llywelyn Welsh resistance virtually ceased. With the death of his brother, Dafydd, captured and ignominiously executed, his quarters

Llewellyn's Stone at
Cilmery, near Builth

48

being sent to Bristol, York, Winchester and Northampton, it ended. Beside the A483 at Cilmery about three miles west of Builth there is now, since 1956 only, a monument to Llywelyn. A circle of thirteen trees, one for each of the old counties of Wales, surrounds a rough-hewn monolith of Gwynedd rock. Slate tablets record, in English and Welsh, that near the spot Llywelyn died. It is an extraordinarily dignified spot, the simple beauty of the monolith comparing very favourably with the more usual ornate memorials.

For their betrayal Giffard and his followers were granted huge estates in England. It was as well the new land was far away. In Wales they were Bradwyr Buallt – the Traitors of Builth – and were hated. Such was the level of hatred that Giffard and some of his men in retaliation rode into Builth once, killing the townsfolk who stood and screamed traitor at them. Later, to try to calm things, Giffard was ordered to repay monies he had sequestered from the locals, as though the return of stolen cash would appease the townsfolk.

Builth castle remained strong after the skirmish, and indeed was never taken, surviving the Glyndwr rebellion. Eventually it was used as a convenient stone quarry and dismantled.

As with the majority of English and Welsh market towns, Builth survived various attempts to reduce it to a ghost town, for in addition to the ravages of battle mentioned above the town was also ravaged by fire and pestilence. The fire is well documented, the town having been completely destroyed on 20 December 1691, a fine Christmas present. William III gave money for its rebuilding, but such was the squandering and misappropriation of the funds that only one house was ever completed with the royal gift. The Black Death had occurred earlier and was so bad that the town was isolated by the surrounding farmers who would allow no local out. To feed the locals the farmers ferried supplies across the Nant-yr-arion, that flows into the Irfon to the west of the town. This compassionate act should not be viewed out of context, however, as the stream is still known as Money Brook, the farmers insisting on the money for the provisions being thrown into the stream to avoid contamination. The idea of water as purifier stays with the town, the wells becoming popular, as with other spas, in the early nineteenth century. In 1830 a Dr Daubeny pointed out, in *Philosophical Transactions*, that the wells, 'though less celebrated, are similar in point of constitution to those of Llandrindod; and being double the strength ought to possess superior qualities.' Two water stations were set up, Glanne and Park, both to the west of the town near the Irfon bridge. The water was recommended for all ills (which spa water was not?) but was especially good for tuberculosis, the liver and kidneys, bronchial and lung afflictions, and children with nettle rash. It came in two-, four- and six-gallon jars, at 1s. 3d. per gallon – and money back on the bottle!

The Wye at Builth
Wells

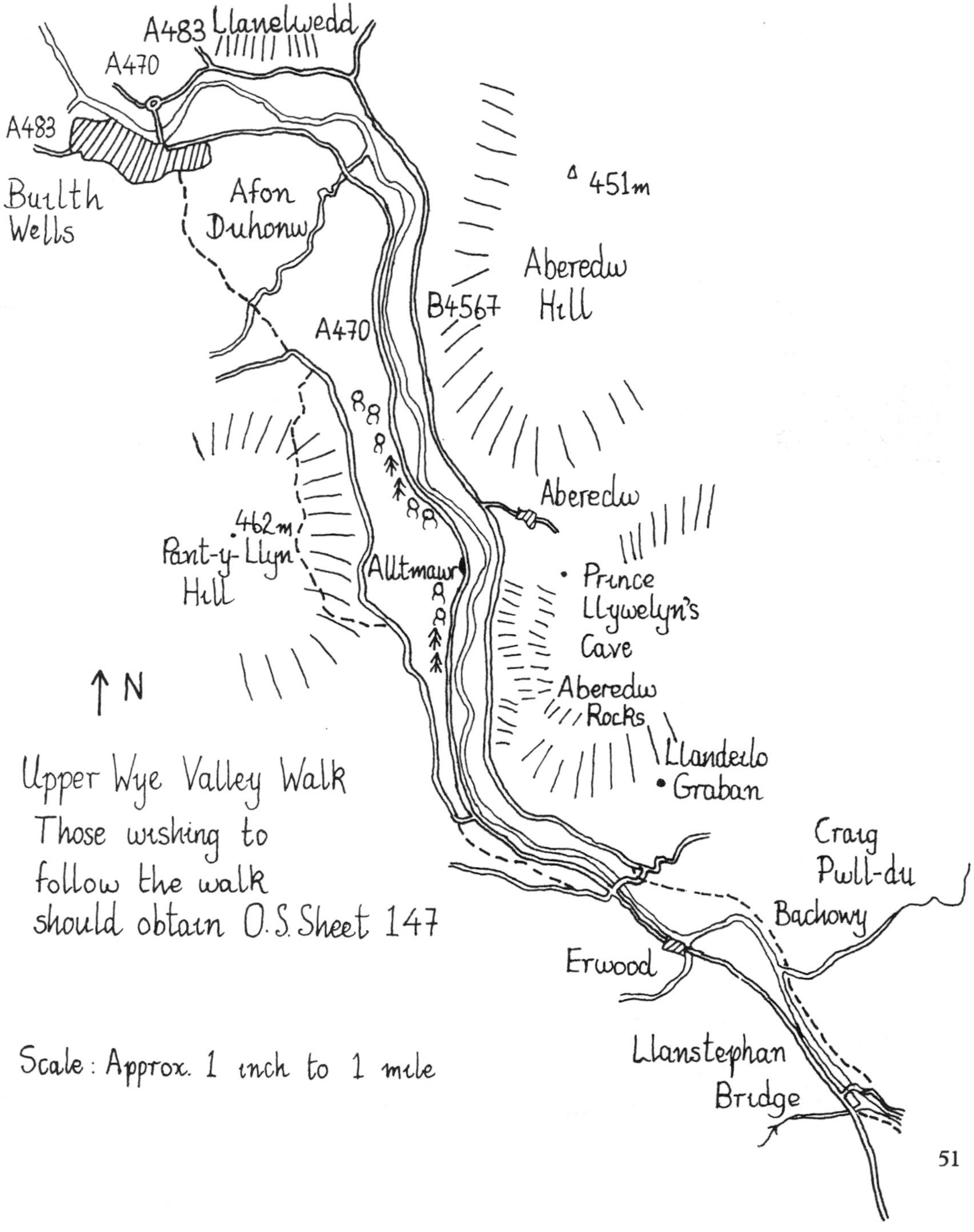

A483 Llanelwedd
A470
A483
Builth Wells
Afon Duhonw
A470
B4567
△ 451m
Aberedw Hill
462m
Pant-y-Llyn Hill
Alltmawr
Aberedw
· Prince Llywelyn's Cave
Aberedw Rocks
Llandeilo
· Graban
Craig Pwll-du
Bachowy
Erwood
Llanstephan Bridge

↑ N

Upper Wye Valley Walk
Those wishing to
follow the walk
should obtain O.S. Sheet 147

Scale: Approx. 1 inch to 1 mile

51

Today the town is an ordinary market town with little of great architectural interest to catch the eye, though the Wye bridge itself is a superb structure. Beside it the Wyeside Arts Centre is an interesting venture, worthy of success. The town is an excellent centre for exploring this very attractive area of mid-Wales or, indeed, the whole of the northern part of the Welsh Wye Valley. Its most notable site is the Royal Welsh Showground to the north of the town, the permanent home of the Royal Welsh Agricultural Society. The site, over 170 acres, is home to the annual show of agriculture and rural crafts.

The Wye Walk leaves Builth eastward on the A470, known as Castle Street, turning right into Castle Road and then left into Newry Road. This is followed 052495 to a bridge, or ford, over the Afon Duhonw.

058488 The track opposite the ford is taken to a minor road which is followed to reach a path off right, which is followed to Pant-y-llyn hill. On the hill, as the path continues around it southward, the views are excellent, both towards Builth, which offers a very good view from above, and across the Wye to the rocks of Aberedw. The latter are the last truly mountainous valley sides that the Wye will have on its journey to the sea, for although it passes the Black Mountains shortly, they offer only a distant backdrop, and the cliffs of the final mile or two are gorges rather than mountain ridges. The rocks here form a remarkable backdrop to the water, strange piled up stone shapes, the whole interspersed with trees to show that the highlands of Wales have indeed gone, and to take the edge off the rugged rocks. The rocks pile up several hundred feet and are a memorable sight from our vantage point high on the opposite valley side.

065463 The Wye Walk continues on the hillside until a lane is joined and followed to the south (right). At the base of the steep hill on this lane, go right along an old 086437 drove road to regain another lane, which is followed to the A470.

The main road has skirted the base of the hill on the west bank of the Wye to gain this spot, passing some of the finest river scenery to be found anywhere in the valley. Indeed this valley section, from east of Builth to Llyswen, ranks with any of the wooded sections further downstream or the mountain section further north. Here the river is wide, but shallow, making small white horses over half submerged rocks that glint in the sunlight filtering through the trees that cover both banks. The water is crystal clear here, the strands of plantain waving in the current and, for the very lucky, the quick flash of a game fish. It is extraordinary that such a beautiful section of river lies only yards from a main road.

Though the A470 is a delightful driving route down this section of the valley, passing, at Alltmawr, one of the smallest churches in Wales, the delightful and quaintly named St Mauritius, it is quieter to follow the B4567 on the opposite bank. To reach that road the driver must follow the A483 from the roundabout at the Royal Welsh Showground as far as Llanelwedd.

52

Near Erwood

Charles Wesley's wife came from here, and he wrote his hymn 'Jesu, lover of my Soul' here to comfort her old nurse as she lay dying. The Wesleys had several connections with the area. John conducted the marriage of Charles and his wife here and preached at Builth church. There he needed a guard and preached outdoors because the incumbent at St Mary's church would not allow him in.

The A481 is taken from Llanelwedd, below the huge quarries that supplied stone for the Elan Valley reservoirs, until the B4567 leads off to the right towards Aberedw village. The village lies at the confluence of the Edw and Wye rivers, the Edw splitting the high ridge on the east bank with a narrow, tree-lined and altogether exquisite valley. It was further up this valley, at Cregrina, that the last recorded wolf in Wales was killed. The fact that it was the last recorded animal does not, of course, mean it was the last one. Did it leave a mate on these hills, pining for its return and dying, a sad and lonely creature? It is easy to see why the locals wanted the wolves eliminated, but such extinctions represent a real problem for the conservationist. Should we reintroduce wolves into Wales and ensure their survival, or take a less dogmatic attitude when the Bengalis decide they are about as happy with wild tigers as the Welsh were about wild wolves?

On a lighter note, the hills here (more correctly the Carneddau above the Llanelwedd quarries) are the source of fossils. One writer, from around the turn of the century, noted with a scientific exactitude that would have made the Royal Society applaud that 'all sorts of prehistoric remains, trilobite fossils and what not' could be found on the hill.

Within the village the famed spot is Prince Llywelyn's Cave, the name given to a hollow, or overhung rock, rather than a true cave, above the church. Legend has it that it was the site of the hermitage of St Cewydd for whom the church is named, but it is for its supposed occupation by Llywelyn that it has achieved fame. There is, however, little evidence that he rested here – more likely the castle closer to the river – and the site is uninspiring. At one stage, around the turn of the century, the cave was gated, the landowner charging for the key. One visitor was suitably incensed by this chaining: 'You need not trouble to enter a place the size of a fowl house!'

Remains of the castle can still be seen, although the site was greatly disturbed by the now defunct railway. When it was occupied, the aesthetic warrior would have been well pleased to have been posted here. Beyond Aberedw the rock outcroppings at the base of Llandeilo Hill are passed before the bridge at Erwood is reached.

Erwood is the anglicized spelling of the Welsh 'Y Rhyd', meaning 'the ford'. The pronunciation has not changed, however, and is a frequent source of surprise to the English who cannot understand where *Air-ooh-d* is! The drovers' road that the Wye Walk has followed to the river crossed it here, the herds moving on to the English border at Rhydspence. It must have been a fine sight, one of the bigger droves, for the drover came not only with cows, but with pigs, sheep and even turkeys. Wales had invented the cowboy several hundred years before Hollywood did.

The village is unspectacular, one of many of its size that can be found throughout Wales, each pleasant enough to while away happy moments without being particularly memorable. Erwood, however, does have a claim to fame, it being here, at the inn, that Henry Mayhew conceived the idea for the magazine *Punch* while hiding from his London creditors. Near the village there is much that is of interest. At Llandeilo Graban, just across the bridge, the last Radnorshire dragon was killed. Those following the river could now turn their trip into a dragon hunt, as we shall also visit Mordiford where the last Herefordshire dragon died. Here the dragon lived in the church tower and made a general nuisance of itself around the neighbourhood running through the usual dragon repertoire. As usual it took an 'ordinary' local to dispose of it, in this case a ploughboy who constructed a 'beast' of wood to which all manner of knives and axes were attached. The boy then put this in with the dragon as it slept; when it awoke and saw the beast, it attacked furiously, cutting itself to pieces on the many blades. It is a feature of dragon stories that they die unpleasantly at the hands of ordinary people. There was obviously a shortage of knights and humane killers in medieval Britain.

Also across the river from Erwood is Craig Pwll-du on the Bach Howey or Bachowy running down to join the Wye. This pool, the name meaning Rock of the Black Pool, is notorious in local mythology. It is said that a castle once stood above the pool and that it was occupied by a cruel chieftain. His main delight was in capturing local maidens and 'ruining' (!) them. Once the ruination was complete he would throw them into the dark pool below. A huge red spot on the rocks beside the pool was said to be the blood of one maiden who unfortunately missed the pool. The red spot also forms part of the legend, however, since it is said that it can only be seen by the faithful.

As if one strange pool in the area was not enough, there is another near here, on Pant-y-llyn Hill above Alltmawr, the hill skirted by the Wye Walk. There, to the west of the summit, is a mountain lake so deep that eight bell ropes tied together did not reach the bottom. Now that may not be the most common of units for measuring lake depth, but it does suggest that the lake is not a shallow one. Those carrying out the measuring, about 200 years ago, were looking for a town said to have been drowned here. Later they dug a trench from the lake in the hope of draining it, but they did not succeed. Some say a thunderstorm directed at them made them realize they should cease, others that a mermaid came out of the water and said they must stop or Builth would be drowned.

Near Erwood

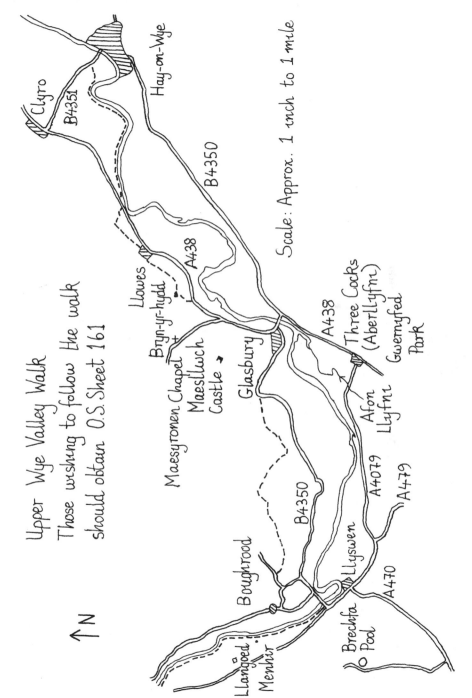

Upper Wye Valley Walk
Those wishing to follow the walk
should obtain O.S. Sheet 161

↑N

Scale: Approx. 1 inch to 1 mile

Clyro
B4351
Hay-on-Wye
B4350
A438
Llowes
Bryn-yr-hydd
Maesyronen Chapel
Maesllwch Castle
Glasbury
A438
Three Cocks (Aberllynfi)
Gwernyfed Park
Afon Llyfni
B4350
A4079
A479
Llyswen
A470
Brechfa Pool
Boughrood
Llangoed Menhir

57

The Wye Walk continues from Erwood by crossing the bridge upstream of the village and following what was the old railway track downstream. The track, and river bank, have here been designated a roadside nature reserve, which is an excellent idea. It is certainly true that the plant life here, particularly the wild flowers, and the insect and, therefore, bird life that collects around it are profuse. The river valley, as with the section upstream of Erwood, is superb and this section of the Walk is as good as any that exists on the river.

The Wye is crossed again at the Llanstephan bridge; follow the western bank to the bridge near Llyswen. Here the walking is right on the Wye bank, so that the river itself holds the interest. But there are other things to observe. About half-way between the bridges, to the right, is Llangoed, inappropriately called a castle by the Ordnance Survey. It is, in fact, a mansion from the early years of this century and is by Sir Clough Williams-Ellis, more famous for Portmeirion further north. Beyond it is a standing stone, some eleven feet high, set upright in the centre of a field. Such stones are of great interest at this time with the fashion for earth magic, but it cannot be denied that they hold a fascination. Wales has many; indeed the popular name *menir* is derived from the Welsh *maen hir*, or long stone, and though these are mainly in more mysterious places, on wild, wind-swept moors, there are few that have been sited in a more aesthetically pleasing spot.

The Walk passes Boughrood (pronounced *Bock-rooh-d* and meaning little ford), a village with two castles, the remains of a Norman building, and a private residence from the early nineteenth century. One owner of the later castle, Francis Fowkes, in the last half of the eighteenth century, had fifteen children by Mary Lowe (said to have been a London actress though it would appear unlikely that she found the time) without bothering to marry her, having made his fortune in India, where he had a son by an Indian woman he also forgot to marry.

Just beyond the bridge that links Boughrood with Llyswen the Wye performs an extraordinary S-bend, coming within yards of itself. At some stage in the future the points will presumably touch, leaving behind a geographically perfect ox-bow lake and separating Llyswen from the river for good. That would be sad, for Llyswen, despite its present humble appearance, has been a famous spot on the Wye bank. The village was named by Roderic, a South Wales prince of the ninth century, who built here a *llys-wen*, a white court or palace, reputedly the finest palace in the whole of Wales. Of this building, nothing now remains. One of the reasons for the decline of the village may have been the splitting up of Roderic's land between his three sons after his death. This division of land between sons was a continual problem for the Welsh when attempting to present a united front against an invader, as it caused fragmentation of the

Gravestone in
Boughrood
churchyard

nation and, invariably, civil war. Roderic decided that his sons should control Powys, North and South Wales, with disputes to be decided at one of three towns. One of these was Llyswen, but as the fragmentation caused endless disputes, none of which could ever be decided by anything except fighting, Llyswen fell into disrepair and disrepute. Now all that remains is a tiny village with a peace exemplified by Brechfa Pool to the west, a sanctuary for all bird life, wild fowl particularly. The Wye Walk crosses the Wye at the Llyswen bridge, visiting Boughrood before making its way by lane and path, at some distance from the river, to Glasbury. Here the Afon Llyfni joins the Wye, having run down from Llangorse Lake set to the west of the Black Mountains. The lake is some way from our river, but is worth considering for an outing. It is a lake of many legends, having been formed by the drowning of a castle or town steeped in evil. Sometimes in rough weather the bells of a fairy church are heard to ring. Perhaps because of the triumph of the good lake waters over the evil stones, the waters of the Afon Llyfni do not mix with them as the river flows through.

From Glasbury, which will be mentioned again below, the Wye Walk continues, with great care being required, along the A438. Through trees to the left, the wayfarer catches glimpses of Maesllwch castle, an imposing structure with a distinctly ancient appearance. Surprisingly, it was built as late as the 1820s. A road, left, is then passed, signed to Maesyronen Chapel. The chapel, dating from the last decade of the seventeenth century, is perhaps the oldest non-conformist chapel in Wales and was established in a farmhouse perhaps 100 years older. There is a legend that Oliver Cromwell preached here.

It is not to Maesyronen that we follow our Walk, which instead goes left about half a mile further on, towards Bryn-yr-hydd and then on to Llowes. This too will be dealt with below. Beyond Llowes the Walk continues to the A438 and crosses it to reach the river which is followed for two miles. Go across to the B4351, turn right and continue to Hay-on-Wye to finish. The route has taken us on a thirty-six-mile tour of the Upper Wye Valley from Rhayader to Hay, exploring at the river side and the valley sides many of the finest aspects of the Wye both scenically and historically. It is an excellent walking route and deserves to become more popular, perhaps eventually competing with the 'prettier', but more populated, Lower Valley Walk that will be mentioned later.

Glasbury, with its old houses and church grouped near a village green, is very English in appearance, evidence of our closeness now to the border. The name, however, is very Welsh, deriving from Clas-yr-Wy, the *clas* by the Wye, yet another early Welsh monastery. The founding monk here was St Cynidr, whose name is also borne by a *llan* further south, and whose grandfather, Brychan, gave his name, Brycheiniog, to the county of Breconshire. The village is the legendary site of a battle between the Welsh and the Saxons, the Saxons being led by Earl Harold, ten years before Hastings, Leofric, the husband of Godiva, and Bishop Leofar, who gave his title, in death, to the rocks of Tarren yr Esgob, the Bishop's rocks, on the Black Mountains a little to the south.

One mile south-west of the village is the Welsh village of Aberllyfni. The coat-of-arms of the Lords of the Manor included a stag, two bells, three spears and three cocks. It is for the latter that the village has been named in English – Three Cocks. The family home, Gwernyfed Park, lies close to the village, a very fine mansion which is now a comprehensive school.

It is downstream from Glasbury that the river becomes public. This means that (as with a public footpath) there is no requirement to consult the riparian owners in order to boat down river. However, it must be remembered that the right to travel over the river does not automatically mean that you have the right to launch or land a boat anywhere, or to camp anywhere on the banks.

On a warm evening in July three canoeists launched their boats from the northern bank of the Wye. Two of us had the perfect training for a canoe trip over the 100 miles to Chepstow: we had made a dozen or so escapes, in a pool, some with spray-decks, but never managed a roll, and had one thirty-minute outing on a lake. Lakes have two distinct advantages: they do not have slopes, and they are very wide. By comparison the third member of our party was very experienced – he had done it all twice. We dispatched our driver, who had the camping gear, to Hay bridge to gauge our progress. Since the river was running at 2 or 3 m.p.h. and we could obviously manage a good walking speed, say 5 or 6 m.p.h., we would be at the bridge, 5½ miles away, in forty minutes or so. In fact he had better get going now.

Just over 2½ hours later our sherpa was anxiously pacing the bridge for the hundredth time. He had been to Glasbury several times, been all the way down to Whitney, paced the bridge some more. And then we arrived. The problems had started very close to Glasbury, when the river swung right suddenly, the current increased surprisingly and my boat, sideways on now, offered my head to the low branch of an overhanging tree. Thereafter I was surprised how narrow the river seemed, one bank or the other always being on the end of the canoe. By the following morning we were managing a steady 4 m.p.h., reaching Bredwardine for lunch, having a carefree, if inexpert and occasionally disastrous, hour at Monnington falls. We were more expert at the Symonds Yat rapids and with sore wrists, swollen unpleasantly and numbed by water-soaked handkerchiefs, Tintern arrived very quickly.

Driftwood, Glasbury

It is not for the fact that I learnt to canoe or shot the falls that I remember the trip. It is for the river itself. The very early morning start that gave perfect calm in the bendy section beyond Clifford, a light mist gently lifting and ducks surprised into early morning flight by our approach; a heron fishing in the shallows oblivious of our presence in its efforts to catch its breakfast; the heat of the day, with the sun dazzling off the water and the air apparently thick with the darting, bright blue damsel-flies; the cool of the early evening on the tree-lined river, shadows dancing on the water. Add to this the laughter as a cry of 'Yes!', signalling success at the Monnington falls, was drowned out, almost literally, by the river as it struck back, and you have the perfect trip.

Llowes village is famous for its *menhir*, a carved standing stone that once stood in the churchyard, but has now been moved into the church. The stone is known by at least two names and forms part of a great number of stories. Factually it is a monolith about 7½ feet high, tapering from three foot at the base to 2¼ feet at the top, a little under one foot thick. Front and back it is decorated, one side with a Celtic wheel cross, the parts patterned, the other with a plain cross. This interpretation, however, is disputed, Hutton, for instance, claiming that the patterned carving was of the British goddess of war, Malaen. The church here is on the site of a *clas* founded by St Meilig, and the stone has frequently been called St Meilig's cross. Since the date of the carving has been given as anything from the sixth to the eleventh century it is possible that Meilig, who arrived here from Clydeside around 650 A.D., did indeed have some hand in the erection of the stone. Many Welsh *menhirs* are much older, and it is also possible that early Christian Celts converted an existing stone to a cross, either as a means of sanctifying an obviously pagan site or out of sheer convenience.

The stone is also known as Moll Wallbee's Stone. The story goes that Moll was rebuilding Hay Castle one night (that is rebuilding it during the course of one night!), when a stone she was carrying to the site fell from her apron and lodged in her shoe. She suffered the inconvenience until, in a fit of annoyance, she tossed it over her shoulder. It landed in Llowes churchyard. Moll must have been some person: when the 3½-ton *menhir* was shifted into the church in 1956 it took quite a few volunteers, including the Llowes Mothers' Union. Many standing stones have similar legends attached to them, with stones thrown by the devil, a giant or, more usually, Arthur. The interesting point about Moll is that she appears to have been real. That is not to say she tossed the stone, of course, but 'Moll' is said to have been the nickname of Maud de St Valery or Maud de Braose, wife of William de Braose of Hay Castle. Maud will be mentioned again at Hay, and here it is sufficient to mention that she seems to have had a sharp tongue, which may have gained her a reputation as a tough lady. In the exquisite phrasing of the day this side of her character led to her being described as 'malapert and stomachful'.

As we have approached Hay we have entered deeper into what is often described as Kilvert country. At Clyro this country has its heart. Robert Francis Kilvert was born on 3 December 1840, one of six children of a Wiltshire rector. He graduated from Oxford and was ordained a priest, serving initially as curate to his father. In 1865 he moved to Clyro, where he spent seven years as curate, the happiest years of his life. He returned to Wiltshire in 1872, moving to St Harmon near Rhayader as vicar in 1876. In 1877 he moved back to the area he loved so much, becoming vicar of Bredwardine. He married in August 1879 but died within a month, of peritonitis. His tombstone suggests that 'he being dead yet speaketh'. In view of the great joy his diary has given readers, this is very apt. The diary covered the period 1870-79 and was contained in twenty-two notebooks, of which only three survive, the rest having been destroyed by his wife and niece who inherited them. Kilvert was a strange man in many ways, a fervent Christian appalled by suffering, yet accepting hunting and being very un-Christian in his attitude to certain people – most notably the French in general, the Parisians ('the scum of the earth') in particular; appalled by a couple living, and loving, in sin and yet having an attitude towards young girls that would raise eyebrows, if not storms, today. In his day Kilvert was beloved of his parishioners, both rich and poor. But so were many other vicars and he would have been forgotten by now were it not for the surviving sections of his diary. These are excellent for their observations on late-nineteenth-century society, its beliefs and prejudices, for the lovely little stories he records – he met a man who saw the Scots Greys marching to Waterloo – and for some quite superb descriptive passages. His descriptions of the River Wye, frost on trees and foxgloves, for example, are extremely memorable.

Clyro, not surprisingly, features in many of his passages. Very early in the diary we learn that a baby was baptised in Clyro church on 13 February 1870 in a font swimming with ice which had been broken so that the service could start. The cold is a recurrent theme. On Christmas Day 1870 Kilvert sat down in his bath on to a sheet of ice which, when it broke, hurt his thighs, the ice cutting like broken glass. May 1872 was 'the bitterest bleakest May I ever saw . . . and out-herods Herod'. In mid-December 1878 the Wye was frozen completely at Moccas, while on Christmas Day the thermometer read 4°F. at Monnington. It is common to maintain that the weather is deteriorating, the summers being wetter and cooler, the winters colder and longer, but are they any worse than the ones Kilvert mentions?

Kilvert's little stories are excellent, cameos of life in Victorian rural society. Some are humorous – like the story of the little boy in Clyro who saw three juicy pears lying in a pit and jumped in to get them. The pit was a cess-pit and the boy was lucky to survive, his calls being heard just as he was about to submerge. He was dragged out, still holding his three pears! Others are old-fashioned – the man who 'cured' his ear-ache by pouring in a hot oil made from eels – or historically interesting – the Clyro women who could remember the stocks and whipping posts being used in the village, and the day when one poor victim of the stocks was freed by a friend with an axe. The whole village promptly made a fire of the pieces and added the whipping post to the blaze so that no one would ever be a victim of the system again.

Kilvert is at his most interesting when describing some of the eccentrics who are so famously British and who seem to have been fairly thick on the ground in his time. The owner of Maesllwch Castle owned a baboon that terrorized anyone who entered the grounds and had a favourite pastime of dropping cats off the castle roof. Best of all, perhaps, is the vicar of Painscastle, three miles north-west of Clyro, known as 'The Solitary'. When he arrived in the village there was no vicarage and he lived in an old cottage. He moved from that, for one reason or another, into three bathing huts, one each for his study, bedroom and kitchen. Eventually these burnt down and he moved into a chicken house. The Solitary was much admired despite the appalling squalor in which he lived, which was instrumental in the burning of his bathing huts and, later, in his being badly burnt himself. Though in the latter incident he received very unpleasant, extensive and painful injuries, he carried on as usual with his work and sick visiting. To ensure that the Word of God reached all his flock he paid tramps to attend a special service on Sunday and provided them with a cooker on which to make hot meals during the course of the service.

A stranger note is sounded by his story of a Frog Woman, a woman whose mother was cursed for calling the children of an unfortunate woman 'young frogs'. The woman was part frog, Kilvert claims, with the head, eyes, mouth, hands and feet of a frog, and hopped about.

For the rest, Clyro is a pleasant village with an ancient pedigree, evidence of Roman habitation as well as the mound that is all that remains of the Norman castle. Towards Hay is a farm, Tir-y-mynach, the Monk's House, which is evidence of a *clas*, or later monastary. The inn, now the Baskerville Arms, but the Swan in Kilvert's day, is named from a later manorial family. There is evidence to suggest that Conan Doyle based *The Hound of the Baskervilles* on the family and that he re-located the action at their request.

To remind the visitor of Kilvert the Society that carries his name has placed a sundial in Llowes churchyard. With its backdrop of the Black Mountains and its emphasis on the times of the day – morning, evening – it is a most fitting memorial.

The Wye at Hay

Hay-on-Wye

The other side of the river from Clyro is Hay-on-Wye, a busy little market town seen to very good effect from the B4351 road that links the two together. The name derives not from any agricultural reference to winter cattle feed, but from the French *haye* or *haie*, an enclosure. It is probable that the enclosure was something quite specific, and that this is why the town is occasionally referred to even now as The Hay. In that respect it bears comparison with The Hague in Holland, the name of which derives from the same root. The Welsh name Y Gelli or Tregelli is from a similar root, *gelli* or *celli* meaning a hedge. This might imply that at some time there were sacred trees near the site, for it is certainly true that there are a large number of sacred wells and stones in the area. One nineteenth-century visitor to the area mentioned this, noting one particular stone where, he maintained, people were sacrificed and their bodies cut up as offerings to the gods of the harvest. He felt that despite its 'terrible and blood-stained' past it should remain. Since the general tenor of his writing was that every second stone in Wales had been for Druidical sacrifice, every hollow in them for blood libation, we can perhaps treat the passage with caution, at least, and not search too hard for the stone.

There were six or seven wells in the town, many of which were credited with magical properties. St Mary's Well saved the church from being razed when a jet of water erupted from it to dowse a fire that had started there. Swan Well was near the old tumulus and, therefore, gave water that was good for 'burial purposes' (!?) as well as sprains. Walk Well held good eye water, which could also be used for laying spirits. In the mid-eighteenth century a Clyro man married a Papist, 'a great folly', and she visited a Hay well to drink in order to obtain power so that 'she could rule over him'. The well was, presumably, Anglican, as we read that she returned 'bedraggled and besmerched'.

The town was sited here because the increasingly wide valley downstream required some strategic position to be maintained where the valley started to narrow. The Normans (who else in this marcher land?) built the first castle and eventually built three at different times, as well as walling the town when King Henry II moved into the area to attempt to restore control over the border barons. It seems extraordinary now that a manorial lord could impose a murage, a tax to build defensive walls, on the locals in order to defy the king, but such was the case. Indeed the area was so independent that it had its own laws. If a Welshman drew a Welshman's blood he had to pay the lord one cow or 5s. – note that it was the lord, not the victim, who benefited.

One notable lord of the manor was William de Braose, whose wife, Maud de St Valery, we have already met at Llowes under the guise of Moll Wallbee.

de Braose was one of the most infamously treacherous of the marcher lords, not noted as a breed for genteel refinement. It was he who invited a Welsh lord to his castle at Abergavenny where he unceremoniously murdered him. This act so appalled Giraldus that, despite his true Norman learnings, he commented on its savagery in the first version of his book 'The Journey through Wales'. Giraldus was Archdeacon of Brecon and, as a result, geographically very close to de Braose. For the second version he omitted the disapproving references. Clearly de Braose had made him an offer he could not refuse.

Following the death of Prince Arthur at the hands of King John, his uncle, the King needed to assure himself of de Braose's continued support. It is likely that de Braose, as a reasonably close associate, knew of the King's actions, and, in addition, had been an Arthur-sympathizer. The King therefore demanded a large sum of money, together with de Braose's children, as ransom. Maud refused to release them, claiming that she would be foolish to give them up to a man who had killed his own nephew. The King was furious, presumably because de Braose had broken a confidence and because Maud had not kept the secret when she had been told. He imprisoned Maud and her sons, probably at Windsor, but possibly at Corfe, William escaping to France. The King demanded de Braose's return, holding the family without food against it. William either did not know of this, or feared for his own fate more than he feared for theirs, and stayed away. Maud and her sons died of starvation, perhaps finally being walled up. Later William died in poverty, although he was buried in Paris.

During the rebellion of Owain Glyndwr the town and castle were destroyed by fire, the castle being declared ruinous. However, accounts were rendered for work on the site in 1453, 3s. 4d. being due for the building of a wall, though thereafter the site was again, and frequently, declared ruinous. In the seventeenth century a fine mansion was built on the site adjacent to the remains, but this too fell into disrepair. Today it is owned by Richard Booth and serves as the headquarters of his book trade. The trade has made Hay the biggest centre for second-hand books in Britain, if not the world, and a walk through the jigsaw puzzle of a town is recommended to avid bibliophiles. Booth is an excellent publicist for the town and, of course, his business. At his insistence Hay has declared a UDI and issued passports.

The association of Hay and books is not new, Kilvert having walked over from Clyro to the annual Book Club Sale. Kilvert also passes on a story that he heard, that a local lady fainted with emotion during a sermon by Mr Welby the vicar. After recounting the story Kilvert notes 'The story is probably untrue.' The church where Welby preached has a fifteenth-century tower, the rest being new, the original having collapsed around the tower around 1700. We can be fairly certain that the collapse was not brought about by the power of one of

Welby's sermons. Religious stone-throwing was also involved in an unsavoury incident when William Seward, who had already been blinded in one eye by a stone at Usk, was stoned to death while preaching outside the Black Lion. He is buried in Cusop churchyard only a mile or so away, but over the border in England.

This closeness to the border between the countries greatly assisted the town in achieving popularity as a market centre. The tolls charged by the town for use of the market in the mid-nineteenth century make interesting reading:

Bull	4d.	Cart hauling merchandise	6d.
Cow or calf	6d.	Waggon hauling merchandise	1s.
Score of pigs	1s. 8d.	Person hawking goods	1d.
Score of sheep	10d.	Basket of vegetables	1d.

The market was, at one stage, hindered by the awfulness of the roads. The roads sank through flooding and over-use of narrow-wheeled waggons. They were levelled by ploughing the edges and throwing the mud into the road centre. The cart-wheel ruts collected water and then the erosion of the mud wore down the level. Eventually the roads were 'so deep that a troop of horses could pass unseen'. The turnpikes that arose to help the situation did nothing of the kind, as we have seen with the Rebecca Riots northward towards Rhayader. History records a further iniquity of the system when a Hay farmer was fined for driving sheep down a non-turnpike lane, it being illegal to avoid the turnpike tolls! Later, when the roads were improved, Hay was a staging centre. Local goods deliveries were also assisted by river transport, the river being just navigable, at high water, up to Hay by flat-bottomed barges. It is said that the church bell, bought from a foundry in Chepstow, was transported here by water in 1740. Within 100 years water transport was assisted by a tramway constructed to carry heavy goods, chiefly coal, which were awkward for the barges and ruined the roads as we have seen. The tramway ran from Brecon where it was linked with the Brecon and Abergavenny canal.

Such transportation was man-made. Giraldus tells us that spiritual transportation also had its place here. He notes that on the night that Henry I died two large pools near the Wye at Hay burst their banks. The water in one, an artificial pond, just ran away as one would expect, but the other, a natural lake, reformed itself two miles away with all its fish and plant life still alive in it. It is puzzling where such stories came from. Were they true? And staying on the subject of miracles, a local tradition has it that fresh sheep's lungs placed on the feet cured pneumonia.

The visitor to the town should not leave without taking a leisurely stroll around it. Remains of the town walls still exist, and the early timber houses of High Town, with its cheese and butter markets, are excellent. The architectural gems are, to the non-expert, a matter of opinion, but do not leave without seeing the Café Royal, dated 1623, and the Three Tuns, from the sixteenth century, in Bridge Street.

To all its charms the town adds, as background, the Black Mountains, named from their sombre appearance. The northern escarpment of this sandstone mass towers above the town, the sky above it sometimes studded with multi-coloured hang-gliders. A road approaches the mountains from the town, moving over Gospel Pass, named because Ss. Peter and Paul came this way at the bequest of Caratacus (the now approved spelling of Caractacus) to preach the gospel to his Silurian tribesmen. Over the pass is the Vale of Ewyas with wonderful mountain gorge scenery and the ruins of Llanthony Priory. The Mountains are worth an outing, the huge whale-back ridges offering excellent walking – but beware of the Old Lady of the Black Mountains, a sinister, spectral figure who leads walkers astray in the mist.

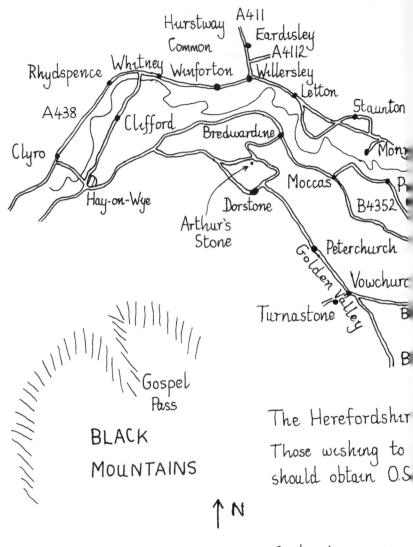

Hurstway
Common

A411

Eardisley

A4112

Rhydspence   Whitney   Winforton   Willersley

Letton

A438

Staunton

Clifford

Breduardine

Clyro

Mon

Moccas

P

Hay-on-Wye

B4352

Dorstone

Arthur's
Stone

Peterchurch

Golden Valley

Vowchur

Turnastone

B

B

BLACK

MOUNTAINS

Gospel
Pass

↑ N

The Herefordshir

Those wishing to

should obtain O.S

Scale : Approx. 1 in

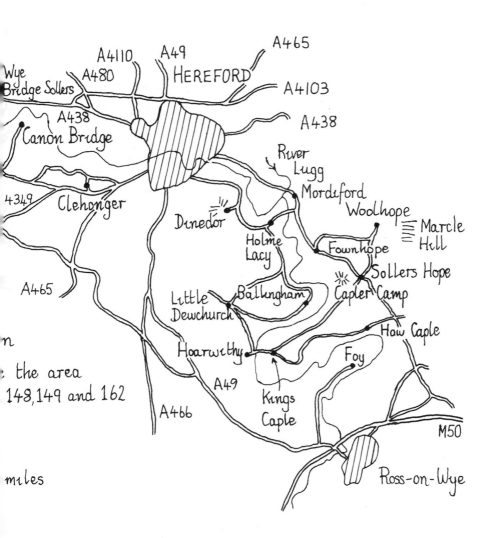

Wye
Bridge Sollers

A4110
A480
A49
HEREFORD
A465

A4103

A438

A438

Canon Bridge

River
Lugg

Mordiford

4349
Clehonger

Dinedor

Woolhope

Marcle
Hill

Holme
Lacy

Fownhope

Sollers Hope

A465

Little
Dewchurch

Ballingham

Capler Camp

How Caple

Hoarwithy

Foy

n

: the area
148,149 and 162

A49

A466

Kings
Caple

M50

miles

Ross-on-Wye

The Plain (from Hay-on-Wye to Ross-on-Wye)

Leaving Hay on the B4350 the visitor crosses the Dulas brook and, in doing so, leaves Wales for England. If instead he or she goes to Clyro and follows the main A438 eastward they will stay in Wales for another three miles, to Rhydspence. Between Hay and Rhydspence the river actually forms the border, the canoeist on this stretch having one paddle blade in Wales, one in England. The river at this point undergoes a subtle change in character, in keeping with the change from Wales to England. We leave a rugged, individualistic, impulsive river in Wales, and reach a calm – dare we say it? – somewhat boring river in England. To the ardent river-watcher the long bends that the river makes through the Herefordshire plain, the banks high and bare, are very different from the straight running river around Builth with its white horses kicking between shallow, tree-lined banks.

I am not saying here that Herefordshire is a boring county. Far from it, it is one of England's most pleasant counties, with scenery to match that of any of the other postcard counties. It is also a remarkably healthy place. In 1609 when James I visited Bacton, a little village in the Golden Valley, he was entertained by a group of twelve Morris Dancers, six of whom were over 100 years old, the rest being over ninety-five. Nor were these ages strange, for 'here is a dozen of yonkers that have hearts of Oak at four score years; backes of steel at fourscore and ten; ribbes of iron at a hundred'. To prove the point, one of the Morrismen married, at ninety-eight, a wife of fifty-two and had a child by her! A healthy pair of yonkers for certain!

On the southern bank the visitor soon reaches Clifford, with the gaunt remains of its castle seen across fields and hedges of bramble. Here, at the ford near the cliff, a castle was built to defend it, and it has become famous as the birthplace of Jane Clifford, Fair Rosamund. It has to be said immediately that Frampton-on-Severn, Hay and another Clifford near Leominster all have a claim to be her birthplace, though popular opinion favours this site. Her nickname came from Rosa Mundi, the Rose of the World, as her beauty was legendary. Her skin was said to have been so white that the blood could be seen moving in the veins beneath it – which is not my idea of beauty. She was seduced by Henry II, reputedly with the help of her governess, and bore him two children before dying, poisoned, so it is said, by Henry's Queen. Her death stops all talk of beauty, as after that the story becomes unpleasant:

> 'It befel that she died and was buried, whyle the Kynge was absent; and whanne he cam agen per grette love, that he had to hyr, he wold se the body in the grave; and whanne the grave was opened, there sate an orrible tode upon her breste bytwene her teetys and a foule addir bigurte her body aboute the middle; and she stank so, that the Kynge ne non other might stande to se that orrible sight. Thenne the Kynge did shette again the grave; and dyde wryte these two veersis upon the grave –
>
> > Here Rose the fair, not Rose the chaste reposes
> > The smell that rises is no smell of Roses.'

It was widely held that the incident was punishment for the open and notorious adultery.

Continuing on from Clifford the visitor crosses the river again, this time at a private toll bridge, not a unique but a far from common sight. To avoid the toll, which is hardly worth avoiding, it is best to go south to Dorstone village, and one of the best prehistoric remains that can be found in the valley, Arthur's Stone.

Dorstone stands at the head of the Golden Valley, which is named from the River Dore in the belief that the name is a corruption of *d'or*, French for 'of gold'. It is not too clear why the Normans chose that name, unless they were impressed, as were subsequent visitors, by the valley in Autumn. The name could also be Welsh, *dwr*, for the much commoner substance water. The village is very pleasant, tucked neatly out of the way of the main road. The church was founded by Richard de Brito, one of the four knights who killed Thomas à Becket. All of the four murderers felt the need to repent the act by building churches or going on pilgrimages. Richard did both, the construction of the church following a fifteen-year penance in the Holy Land. It was held, at a later time, that on the Eve of All Souls the Devil used the church to read a list of those parishioners who would die in the next twelve months for sins they had committed. One local, known as Jack of France, wanting to know the names for personal gain, hid in the church and spied on the Devil as he read. To his horror he heard his own name read out, his sin being spying in church! He repented, prayed hard, but all to no avail, within the year he was dead.

Those with time should follow the Golden Valley, it is full of interest. Do not

Arthur's Stone

miss Peterchurch or the twin churches of Vowchurch and Turnastone. The latter was constructed, so legend has it, by two warring sisters, one of whom declared: 'I vow I shall finish my church before you turn a stone on yours.'

Those with little time should visit Arthur's Stone on their way to Bredwardine. The stone is, in fact, Herefordshire's only *cromlech*, the remains of a Neolithic chambered tomb built between 6,000 and 7,000 years ago. What we see today is the burial chamber itself, which would have been covered, when in use, by a mound, here some eightyfive feet long. Such tombs are among the oldest man-made constructions to be found in Britain. They point to a way of life that had the permanence to allow such a structure to be worthwhile and the 'leisure' time, or wealth, to create it. The sites were chosen so that the tombs could be seen – they were meant to be visible memorials, an imposing feature on the landscape. Their builders had an aesthetic sense, some of the dead having been buried with beads or especially fine pebbles. It is a measure of our affluence today that we can afford more than pebbles to adorn our dead, but it is no sign of our being any more respectful or caring. Such sites are intensely magnetic. Stand alone here as night falls and try hard *not* to feel a common bond with a sentient being a few millenia ago. It would not be easy.

The name of the site is a late romantic touch. Earlier the site was Thor's Stein – which could also explain Thorstone, corrupted to Dorstone, in the valley below, were not its site in the Dore valley to offer an alternative explanation – but the locals obviously preferred a Celtic hero to a Norse god.

From Arthur's Stone, a minor road drops down steeply to Bredwardine, the final parish of the Rev. Francis Kilvert, and the site of his grave. Kilvert became vicar here in 1877, returned here after his marriage and died here. We have seen that his great love was Clyro, but he must also have liked this village, for the river scenery here, and for the next short section to Moccas, is very similar to that above Hay. Kilvert lies in the churchyard under a white cross. Unusually, his wife does not lie beside him, there having been no room, and she lies in the new churchyard the other side of the church lane.

The church is a pleasant building with some Norman work, but most from much later. One very fine piece inside is an alabaster effigy believed to be of Sir Roger Vaughan, a Lord of the Manor killed at Agincourt. Vaughan's father-in-law, Sir Davy Gam, was also killed at that battle, having intercepted a blow meant for Henry V and been knighted for his action as he lay dying. Gam was a Welshman and a larger-than-life figure. He attempted to kill Owain Glyndwr at his parliament in Machynlleth and was very lucky to have escaped death for this. When asked at Agincourt by Henry how many Frenchmen there were, he replied that there were enough to kill, to take prisoner and to run away. So admired was he that Shakespeare modelled Fluellen on him.

The churchyard has become the focal point of pilgrimages by lovers of Kilvert's work, but the real focus of his writings is the countryside and, therefore, the river. From the churchyard there is a very fine walk to the bridge, first passing the Old Vicarage that has been very little altered since Kilvert's time even though it is no longer the vicarage. Beyond is the river and then a very fine bridge of six arches with the roadway thirty feet above the river. If that differential seems excessive, it is worth remembering that Bridge Cottage, the old toll house on the village side of the bridge, was almost submerged by the river in 1963 when it rose twenty feet in as many hours. The bridge is well separated from the main village, as indeed is the church, but it is worth the extra walk if only to see the Red Lion, a very fine seventeenth-century inn.

And after the walk a return, perhaps, to the churchyard. On the Sunday before Kilvert died the church bell struck as if made of lead, and at his funeral the coffin was carried under arches of flowers erected by the parishioners to welcome the honeymoon couple home. He was well loved even then for the gentleness that pervades his writing.

The visitor to Hay who continues to Hereford on the A438 soon passes Rhydspence Inn, the first, and last, inn in England and much beloved for that reason by the drovers. At that time it was the Cattle Inn, an appropriate name. As well as stopping here for a well-earned drink, the drovers took advantage of the considerable skills of a local blacksmith, who would shoe the cattle in preparation for the hard roads of England. To do this the man would turn the cattle on their backs, attaching a two-part shoe to each hoof. The job was, not surprisingly, dangerous as well as requiring great strength. The present inn is architecturally striking, a fine black-and-white timbered building, and there was a time when it was not alone. Kilvert passed through the hamlet once at midnight, noting that the English inn was ablaze with light and noisy with revellers, while the Welsh inn was dark and silent. He also noted – though earlier, so it cannot necessarily be seen as retribution – that a particularly savage summer flood had swept away pigs, sheep, hay and roads and put 'four inches of mud in the Rhydspence Inn on the Welsh side of the border.'

Beyond Rhydspence is England, the Herefordshire plain where the twisting Wye is, following Kilvert, a silver serpent in the early morning light. Strung out along it here are a collection of interesting villages and hamlets. First is Whitney, named from the saxon Witenei. Since this means, apparently, 'clear water stream with boggy islands', it shows how wonderfully economical the Saxon language was. Now Whitney has its toll bridge only, the latest in a succession of flood-destroyed structures, though once it had a railway bridge as well, the ramparts of which still lurk below the water to snatch at the unwary canoeist.

Bredwardine bridge

Below Whitney the meandering river has created some very deep pools, which have acquired names from the salmon fishermen. Here are Locksters, Old Court and the Cowpond. The latter, said to be forty foot deep, yielded Doreen Davey the record Wye salmon of 59½ pounds in 1923. The fish was 52½ inches long, 29 inches around.

The next village is Winforton, near which St Cynidr of Glasbury lived as a hermit. It is a village of truly Herefordshire appearance with its timber-framed houses. Note especially the very fine Court.

Beyond Winforton is Willersley, a hamlet easily missed if you blink, distinctly less worthy of note than Eardisley, a little north, that boasts a castle mound, an exquisitely carved and very ancient font in the church, and an oak tree thirty feet around and over one hundred feet high on Hurstway Common.

Next is Letton, flooded so badly over the years that the area around it has become known as Letton lakes. One inhabitant said of the awful floods of 1795 that the water was four feet higher in the church nave than he could ever remember before! A little way north is Waterloo, which suggests a macabre sense of humour or pessimistic acceptance of fate.

South-east of Letton the A438 is joined by the lane from Bredwardine bridge, and again the traveller has a choice of banks. The canoeist has no such problems and is rewarded in this next section by some interesting water and views. After the long sweeping left-hand bend beyond Bredwardine, the canoeist swings right to face the Brobury Scar, a sandstone cliff on the left below which there are a number of large boulders in the water. Depending upon river level these can offer some points of minor interest or some show-stopping crunches. Beyond the Scar there is a quiet, peaceful section of river with a very fine view to Moccas Court on the bank top to the right. The quiet and peace are then soon over, the paddler coming upon a notice suggesting that he stop and walk down to inspect Monnington falls. Again the excitement is dependent upon water level, because a straightforward passage can be found to the right of the falls if the rock pavement is covered. The falls themselves are a sharp fall into a narrow and swift-running channel, with most of the work being over after the canoe has been lined up. Then it's a dip here, pull there and whoosh! it's over. Alternatively you are. One member of our team lost one-nil to the river on his first try, emerging from the channel wet but undaunted, declaring that he had it sorted out now, it would be O.K. next time. So he had another go and the river was now two-nil up. Eventually he got it right.

By road, on the northern bank, Brobury is reached from Letton, now a deserted hamlet but offering a good starting point for a walk past the Scar and down to Monnington and from there on to Byford. The final approach to Monnington is along the Monnington Walk, a glorious avenue of trees, said to

Staunton-on-Wye
church

have been planted in 1660 to celebrate the Restoration. Kilvert loved this walk, referring to it as the Royal Walk, perhaps in keeping with the celebration planting, perhaps from its royal nature.

Nearer the main road, but still away from it, is Staunton-on-Wye, a long straggling village, not as pretty as some others but with fine views to the south. It was here that the cattle signalled Christmas one year, according to Kilvert. He had not seen it, but the friend of a friend had. This man was at Staunton on Christmas Eve, and at the stroke of midnight those cattle that were standing knelt, and those that were lying rose to their knees. They all then moaned gently, tears running down their faces.

Next village to the east is Monnington, a wonderful spot. The village is famous as the last resting place of Owain Glyndwr, but a complex web of half-truths has created this fame. Glyndwr was never finally defeated in his rebellion. The rebellion started in 1400, reaching its high point in 1405 when the Welsh and their French allies invaded England, but thereafter fell away. There was never a decisive battle, a series of small victories by the English, and the capture of strategic castles, meaning that the Welsh were deprived of a base and, ultimately, of the stamina to continue the fight. By 1410 the rebellion was, effectively, over. By 1415 the English king was so confident of his position that he could offer Glyndwr, who had not been captured, a free pardon. The offer was refused, or, rather, never accepted. It is widely believed that by 1417 Glyndwr, who would by then have been about sixty years old, was dead. His final years are shrouded in mystery. One story has him living out his days with his daughter Alice and her husband John Scudamore at their manor at Monnington Straddel in the Golden Valley. Another story has him living out his days with a daughter, variously called Anne, Janet or Margaret, who married Sir Richard Monnington of Sarnesfield. Ignoring the problem of what Sir Richard's wife was actually called, it can be seen where confusion over the name Monnington arose. It may well be that there would never have been a connection with the village here had it not been for an accident in 1679. Then, during rebuilding work on the church, a sycamore tree was removed, and beneath it was a stone coffin containing a skeleton. Someone who knew that there was a connection between Glyndwr and Monnington suggested it was the prince, and the story stuck. The stone lid of the coffin, now broken, can still be seen to the west of the porch. Once the story had started it was easily embroidered. One writer, earlier this century, has Glyndwr dying at the Court on 20 September 1415. The Court is actually 200 years younger than that, and even if a previous building can be argued, such an exact date is without foundation.

The church, with its stone grave slab – which covered someone's body, that someone having been ignored in the scrambling for a prince – has the finest approach of any in the Wye Valley. It is a green lane, at first down an avenue of cherry trees planted for the 1977 Silver Jubilee that is in keeping with the Royal Walk mentioned above. In wet weather this grass track might be less appealing, but when it is dry it could not be improved. The church itself is a delightful building. The west tower is early thirteenth century, but the rest is from the last quarter of the seventeenth century and, being complete, is an excellent example of its type. It contains a memorial for Francis Perrott, who served the Venetian Republic against the Barbary pirates, while in the yard is the grave of William Williams, who fought in the Peninsular War and at Waterloo, returning unscathed to die in his native village at the age of eightysix. Clearly Monnington was a lucky place to be born if you wanted to fight battles and die of old age. Beside the church is Monnington Court, where Glyndwr almost certainly did not die, as fine an English country house as will be seen anywhere, beautifully fronted by water.

The water is not the Wye, though it links up with it. The Wye itself at this point has the falls already mentioned, around which the flat-bottomed barges were dragged by winch and muscle power.

At the other end of the walk from Monnington is Byford, which was once an important river crossing with two ferries, one that carried animals – horses and cattle – and another that carried 'footmen and such sort.'

Beyond Byford is Bridge Sollers, where the Wye can be crossed again, and which offers a very fine view of the Black Mountains. The village has a Norman church, which should be visited to see the carvings on the imposts of the doorway. There one dragon watches you as you stare at it, while two others appear to be crawling out of a man's head intent on nibbling his ears. At Bridge Sollers bridge visitors who have kept to the southern bank will rejoin the river. They will have passed Moccas, a strangely named spot consisting mainly of a Court, best seen from the river, and a deer park.

In the late fifth century AD, the King of Ertychi (now Archenfield), one Pepiau (or was it Clavarauc?), found that his daughter, or perhaps granddaughter, Eurdil was pregnant. He attempted to drown her for her shamelessness, and when this failed he had her burnt at the stake on the Wye banks. One story has it that her son was born in the fire itself, another that she was miraculousy saved from death to give birth. Her son was St Dubricius, one-time Bishop of Hereford, who crowned King Arthur at Cirencester in 506 AD. This saintly man founded a religious college near Ross-on-Wye, and from there he was led to another holy spot by a white sow with a litter of pigs. He called the spot Mochros, the place of the pigs. Dubricius died on Bardsey Island and was taken to Llandaff for burial. As he was buried, there was a rainstorm that ended a seven-week drought.

Dusk, near Eaton
Bishop

Moccas Court was built by a local to the design of Robert Adam around 1780. The gardens were laid out by Capability Brown and Humphrey Repton. In them stands a Norman church built of tufa, calcium carbonate, looking a little like concrete blocks. It contains many memorials to the Cornewall family, local lords, including one to seventeen-year-old Mary Jane Cornewall, 'lamentably drowned in the river Wye' in 1839. That placid slow-moving water below the Court cannot be treated with anything but caution. The most famous Cornewall was James, who commanded the *Marlborough* in action off of Toulon in 1743. Both his legs were shot off, but he continued to fight 'upon his stumps.' Not surprisingly, this continuation, and James, were short-lived. He is buried in Westminster Abbey, where the first monument to a naval hero was erected in 1756.

The deer park across the road from the Court is famous for its oak trees, about which Kilvert was lyrical over a century ago. The oaks are, perhaps as a result of Kilvert, more famous than the deer, a form of fallow known as menils with pale markings on their rumps.

East of Moccas is Preston-on-Wye, near which the river makes an impressive S-bend. At points like this, and there are several near here, and again below Ross, the canoeist who has a map can be forgiven for wondering whether it would be worthwhile carrying his boat across half a mile of field rather than paddling several times that distance to reach the same point. Kilvert mentions a talk with the Vicar of Preston, who had decided to move the church to the village green so that it would be closer to the people and to the 'old-tree.' His ambition is to be commended, though the plan never reached fruition.

Staying on the southern bank of the river, the narrow lanes that sometimes come very close to the river can be used to reach Hereford. The visitor will pass Canon Bridge, where logs were built up into rafts for floating downstream to Chepstow, and Eaton Bishop, now almost a suburb of Hereford, with an Iron Age hill fort set on a spit of land above the river. It is very likely that the fort is here because the river afforded protection on one side, rather than as protection of a river crossing. Beyond Eaton Bishop is Clehanger, known as Clunger locally, whose church contains very fine brasses of Sir John Barre, who died in 1483, and his wife. He has his head against his helmet while she is swaying towards him, a goose or swan pulling at her dress. Beyond Clunger is Belmont Abbey, built in the grounds of Belmont House, a house never finished completely because of the money spent on building the Benedictine church. The owners were famous in the area for the paddle steamer which they used for outings on the Wye. The steamer had been brought to Hereford by barge, on the Gloucester-Hereford canal, an ironic means of transport for a boat.

North of the river the city of Hereford is reached by the main A438 from

After January floods,
near Breinton

Bridge Sollers. To the west of that village the main road follows a Roman road, but this went north of the A438 just beyond Monnington, going through Bishopstone to Kentchester, the Roman town of Magnis. At Bishopstone, just north of Bridge Sollers, a very fine mosaic pavement was discovered in a Roman villa while excavating a site for the building of the rectory in 1812. Now only drawings of the pavement exist. Wordsworth wrote a sonnet about the villa. It was not one of his best. The poet lived, at one time, at Brinsop Court, a couple of miles to the north-east. He appears to have liked the Wye, several of his lines being frequently used by writers on the area, and was in the habit of claiming that the section he was currently viewing was the loveliest piece of scenery in England. Many of us have similar difficulty in deciding which is the section we actually place top of our list.

The Roman road, as we have said, went to Kentchester, which was a town proper as opposed to a fortress town. It was a large and important site, certainly the largest on the Wye, and probably grew here because of an earlier settlement on the hill, Credenhill, to the north-east. Although that site was originally Iron Age, the Romans never missed an opportunity of using a well-fortified position.

Leland, the mid-sixteenth-century traveller, is excellent on Kentchester, his mixture of old English and eccentric spelling adding great charm to the site:

> 'This towne is far more auncyent than Hereford and was celebrated yn the Remaynes tyme as appereth by many thinges, and especyally by antique mony of the Caesars, very often fownd withyn the toune and yn ploughyng abowt; the which the people ther cawlleth Dwarfas Mony...
> Traces of the walles and turrets yet appere, prope fundamenta, and more should have appered if the people of Hereford towne and other thereabout had not yn tymes paste pulled doune muche and pyked owt of the best for their buildings...The place wher the toun was ys al overgrowen with brambles, hasylles and lyke shrubbes.'

One of the things I find remarkable about such ancient sites is the amazing wealth of information that is available about them. For instance it is known that in the town at one time Aurelius Polychronidus was selling ointments for eye disorders.

Credenhill, the village beneath the great Iron Age hill fort, where Thomas Treherne, whose poetry was lost for 200 years, was vicar around 1665, lies beyond Kentchester. It was here, in 1887, that one H.P. Bulmer, the son of the rector, started making cider.

On the other side of the A438 from Kentchester the National Trust has a garden, New Weir, a fine place in spring and summer. Eastward a series of minor roads allow the visitor to reach water again for the last time before

Hereford. The drive over the Common and through the village of Breinton is very worthwhile. The river here is at its elegant best again, occasionally tree-lined and moving with gentle meanders rather than tight curves. It was here that the largest fish, a sturgeon, ever taken in the Wye was landed. But not with rod and line, or even net. As befits a monster, a man on the bank stripped off, dived in and fought it hand to fin, knife against whatever the fish had to offer. When the man hauled it ashore it measured 8 foot 6 inches, and weighed 167 pounds.

Hereford

Hereford means in Saxon 'ford of the army', and was an important site but, apparently, not important enough to merit a bridge. The town was a capital of Saxon Mercia but achieved more considerable status after King Offa, of dyke fame, endowed a church here. Offa had his palace at Sutton Walls and invited Ethelbert, his under-king in East Anglia, to it, to marry his daughter Elfrida. Offa's queen was opposed to the marriage and persuaded Offa that the under-king posed a threat to his authority. While a guest at the palace Offa therefore murdered Ethelbert, beheading him – probably, in view of later events – or suffocating him with a pillow. Ethelbert was buried on the banks of the River Lugg and at his burial a column of light brighter than the sun shone from the grave. Three days later the dead king's ghost appeared to one Brithfrid, who was told to take the body to Stratus Waye, that is Hereford. On the way many miracles occurred, including one which implies real carelessness on the part of the bearers. Ethelbert's head was dropped and rolled to the feet of a blind man, who immediately regained his sight. Now it must be admitted that regaining one's sight is great good fortune, but when the first thing you see is a three-day-old, severed head . . . Offa was so afraid of the miracles and of what he had done that he gave one-tenth of all he owned to endow a church, dedicated to St Ethelbert, here. Quendreda, his queen, died within two months, and Elfrida spent her life in a nunnery.

The town was still small, perhaps as few as 100 inhabitants, when, in 1055, Gryffyth, Prince of Wales, and Algar, the disgraced Earl of Chester, banished by Edward the Confessor, fought Ralph, the Governor of Herefordshire, outside the city. The English were defeated, the nobles in the army seeking sanctuary in the cathedral church. The Welsh advanced on it and were met by Bishop Leofgar, who asked that its sacredness be recognized. The Welsh would not yield, all the nobles inside and many townsfolk being killed. The church and town were fired and Leofgar was taken to Glasbury, where he was tortured and killed. Earl Harold, sent to quell the riot, probably constructed the town's first castle. The

Hereford Cathedral

death toll in the first battle was, it is thought, about 500. In an age accustomed to 'mega-death', this seems trivial, but it represented five times the town's population and must have horrified the locals.

The town received its first Charter (allowing it to collect tolls at markets and the bridge) at the time of Richard I, but this caused acrimony with the church, who were at that time accustomed to receiving all major monetary benefactions. There was feuding between the church and citizens for some time. Matters came to a head when the city council issued a writ against a citizen, who hid within the cathedral precincts. The mayor's sergeant advanced to serve the writ and was punched by a canon. Reconciliation was required and occurred in time-honoured fashion the next day. The sergeant and canon shook hands; the canon handed over 6s. 8d. as a fine/recompense; on the mayor's orders the sergeant handed back 5s; the 1s. 8d. was used to oil the wheels of diplomacy in the local tavern.

The castle, another that was 'one of the fayrest, largest and strongest castels in England', stood on Castle Green, although all trace of it has now been erased. Before its eventual disappearance about 250 years ago it had helped Hereford to achieve national, if transitory, fame. It was here that Simon de Montfort held Prince Edward captive. And it was from here that the prince escaped, having asked for a horse to go riding and been given one that could outride his captors. It was from Hereford that Simon later marched to his army's defeat and his own death at Evesham.

In keeping with its place in such morbid events, Hereford also witnessed at first hand some medieval savagery. In 1290 a Welsh chief was executed here, and 'in order to strike terror through the country, was drawn to the place of execution at the tails of horses, and hanged with two companions'. Another example of judicial killing 'to encourage the others', as Voltaire put it. A little later Hugh de Spencer (or Dispencer) was hanged in the market-place on a gallows fifty feet high. He was crowned with nettles and carted around the town bearing a placard with the first six verses of Psalm 52 on it. He was so hated that the townsfolk lost no opportunity in pointing this out to him, and 'never before was so horrid a noise heard against any great person'. It is an unpleasant story, but I can never mention Dispencer without a smile of memory at the description of him as 'the well-known chemist'.

After so much bloodshed the town survived the Civil War unscathed, having fallen to a surprise attack by Col. Birch's Parliamentarian army. The town had held out for some time against the army, which was mainly Scottish and well-feared, but capitulated after 150 armed men got in through the town gates. It seems that half-a-dozen men approached the city, said they were labourers and asked for the gate to be opened. It was. The Scots duly obliged the locals by acting out their worst fantasies, even to the point of dancing in the cathedral to the organ music during the services. All Royalist supporters in the town were fined heavily, perhaps a small price to pay for having chosen the wrong side. There was some local 'told-you-so', for when the king raised his standard at Nottingham early in the war, it had promptly fallen down, which was thought by many to have been a bad omen.

Since we have spoken of the cathedral, or at least of its dedication, it is appropriate to deal with it more fully. Everyone who has been to more than one English cathedral will have his own opinion of the finest view of any of them. I am willing to place my head on the block and record that, while I have not seen every English cathedral, the view of the cathedral church of St Mary the Virgin and St Ethelbert the King across the Wye from Hereford old bridge is the finest in the country. Sadly, at the time of writing, the view is not improved by scaffolding on the tower, but that is a small price to pay for the continued existence of the church.

The earliest recorded church in stone on the site was built early in the eleventh century by Athelstan, the present building having been started later. The age of the main fabric dates mainly from later periods, the cathedral having been rebuilt, extended and restored almost continuously. The west front is, for instance, only 200 years old, the original having collapsed. Inside, the building houses the tombs of many of the bishops, the most famous having been Thomas de Cantilupe who was bishop in 1275-82 and canonized in 1320. He was a man 'who sucked in sanctity with his milk,' beloved of his flock for his humility and kindness, but tough in negotiations with the Archbishop of Canterbury over the rights of the see. So tough was he that he was excommunicated in 1282 and travelled to Italy to plead his case with the Pope. Unfortunately he died at Orvieto. His heart was removed and sent to the Earl of Cornwall at Ashbridge, Buckinghamshire, and his bones were sent back to Hereford after the flesh had been boiled off them. This all seems a bit gruesome, and for those that carried out the work it must have been. However, the idea of heart burial separate from other bits was not new. At a time when the nobles frequently had land in more than one place, they were often carved up and distributed for burial.

Almost immediately after the bones were deposited in a shrine in the cathedral, miracles were claimed for them. Over 300 people were cured of various afflictions and the church was so inundated with candles from pilgrims to the site that they represented a sizeable treasure and sparked off arguments among officials over the distribution of the windfall. It was said that sixtysix men and women were raised from the dead as a result of prayers at the shrine. Interestingly, some of these had been executed as criminals, though it is not clear whether St Thomas only revived the innocent. The shrine was so famous that Edward I sent his falcons here to be cured when they developed the raptorial equivalent of fowl

Corner of the
Cathedral Close,
Hereford

Hereford from
Victoria Bridge

pest. It presumably worked, too, as later he sent them again. Finally, after 420 accredited miracles, Thomas was canonized.

Even that was not the end of the miracles. In 1340 the Black Death killed many townsfolk. But the plague departed swiftly when the relics of St Thomas were carried in procession around the town. This event forms a link with the White Cross that those who have entered Hereford by main road from the west will have seen. There are two versions of why the original of this cross was erected. The most likely is that it marks the spot to which the market was moved when the plague came, local farmers not wanting to enter the town. But it was also said that a cross was erected here by St Thomas for a miracle he witnessed when he paused to view the cathedral and the bells started to ring without human agency. As always, the existence of a shrine associated with miraculous cures brought in many pilgrims, and considerable wealth for the church and bishop. A later bishop ordered, for one day's eating, one boar, ten oxen, eight porkers, sixty fowls, thirteen fat deer and 900 eggs. We learn that 'he derived much benefit from drinking water'. It is doubtful whether simple and honest St Thomas would have approved.

Within the cathedral there is much that is very fine, and not all of that the famous pieces. The cloisters are almost perfectly preserved and some of the memorial brasses need careful studying. They include St Ethelbert, his head in his lap, and a whole range from the fourteenth and fifteenth centuries. It is undeniable, however, that the majority of visitors wish to see the Mappa Mundi and the chained library. The former is a map of the world, on vellum, made by Richard de Bello around the end of the thirteenth century. It is artistically and historically of great interest, but cartographically awful. The world is flat, of course, with Jerusalem at its centre, and is based on the Biblical world. Adam and Eve appear twice, once in and once out of the Garden of Eden, in Asia, and there are numerous other direct Biblical references. In Britain the rivers are well represented and include our river, the Wie. The chained library contains 1,444 books, each with a chain attached to the front edge of the cover. It represents the largest library of its type in the world and is of enormous value to antiquarians. There are two pages of seventh-century script from St Matthew's Gospel, and 227 other manuscripts dating from the eighth century onwards. The manuscripts include works on sheep-skin parchment, the skins prepared by polishing with pumice and whitening with chalk. The printed books include two by Caxton. It is ironic now to think that when the manuscripts and books were all in a room of the Vicar's 'college', or rooms, in 1842, the dean requested that it be moved. If it was not, he warned that all 'the rubbish' would be taken out and burnt!

On the subject of famous things and famous people, Hereford has been home to several. In Pipe Lane Eleanor Gwynn was born, a lady who achieved fame as Nell Gwynn, mistress of Charles II. A grandchild of hers, Lord James Beauclerk, was a Bishop of Hereford. Since, at one time anyway, Nell was an actress, it is reasonable to mention that David Garrick, England's most famous actor, was also born here, though by chance only, as his father, a serving soldier, was stationed nearby. Perhaps the city's best-known association with the arts is that Sir Edward Elgar lived here when he was knighted. He assisted with the Three Choirs Festival for which the city is still famous. This annual event takes place, in rotation, between the cathedrals of Hereford, Gloucester and Worcester. In the 1902 festival Elgar's *Dream of Gerontius* was premiered, and it is now played on the last night of each festival.

It is not possible in the scope of one book to give every place on the river the words it deserves. In the case of Hereford, its history, its cathedral and its architecture, a complete book would only just be sufficient. But to acquire the feel of the place, and perhaps to stimulate a desire to return, it is best to walk around it. To assist the visitor in such a walk, the tourist association have produced two reasonably priced leaflets, one on a river walk, one on a town walk.

The river walk starts below the Castle Green, with its own Nelson's Column, at the Victoria Bridge, a lovely little suspension bridge built for Queen Victoria's Diamond Jubilee. From here the town and cathedral can be seen well, but it is at the old, or Wye, bridge that I contend the best view is to be had. It is said that a visiting bishop once said to the Bishop of Hereford: 'If you will give me your river I will give you my see.'

Near the bridge is a small wharf, evidence of Hereford's ancient and seemingly ridiculous trade of ship-building. The river has always been important to the town. Not only in terms of trade and industry – it was once written into the indentures of town apprentices that they should not eat salmon more than 'thrice weekly.' That fish, now such a high-priced luxury, was once so common it almost came with six penn'orth of chips.

The river walk ends at the Broomy Hill Museum, a Victorian waterworks and collection of water pumps. It is one of several museums in the town, which has readily, and in very welcome style, embraced its past. Do not miss the Bulmer Museum of Cider near the magnificent metal-work woodpecker, emblem of the Bulmers Company. It is difficult to ignore cider around here, as there are several old cider presses as memorials. Even one of the garages has one on the forecourt.

The town walk, also known as the 'principal walk' as that was how it was described in a guide of 1806, visits the major features of the old town, including Old House, the most photographed house in the county. In fairness, it is a beautiful timbered, gabled house now set, somewhat incongruously, in the main shopping centre. It also passes the church of St Peter, in front of which is a statue of Sir George Cornewall Lewis credited with the saying: 'Life would be tolerable, but for its pleasures.' This sounds (and is?) profound, but I find it incomprehensible.

Near to both Old House and the statue is High Town, the original market, for Hereford was, and is, a market town. The produce has changed a little over the years. The *Hereford Times* of 1876 noted wife-selling in the market, a trade legal enough to be taxed, and you cannot get more legal than that. The report noted that the wife had a halter, and that when bartering was complete she was led away by her new owner (husband?) on a lead.

We, too, must take our leave of Hereford to continue our meanderings down river to the sea. It is tempting to take a 'Kemble pipe', the Hereford expression for one for the road. It is an expression based, sadly, on a tragic tale. In 1679 John Kemble the Roman Catholic priest of St Weonard was sentenced to death as a recusant. He was over eighty at the time and seems to have been very calm, even though advanced years cannot make hanging look attractive. When Mr Digger, the under-sheriff, came for him, Kemble asked for time to pray and smoke his pipe. Mr Digger agreed and when Kemble lit his pipe, the sheriff lit his own. Kemble finished his pipe, drank a glass of wine and said he was ready to go. Mr Digger had not finished his pipe, however, and asked if he might be allowed to do so. Kemble agreed and when Digger had finished, the two men walked out together. The execution was here at Hereford.

On leaving Hereford the Wye-follower can again choose a bank. On the northern side the B4224 passes through Hampton Bishop, a pleasant village with a good Norman church, before reaching Mordiford. Strictly Mordiford is on the River Lugg, a few hundred yards from its confluence with the Wye, but is worth visiting as the home of Herefordshire's last dragon. One day a young girl, Maud, out looking for blackberries found the dragon, a sweet, cucumber-sized creature in the grass. There are some suggestions that it was amphibious and had been left behind by a high river. Maud took it home, where her father, horror-stricken, said he would kill it. Maud was tearful and so her father said she could keep it, planning to get up early to get rid of it. Maud, a suspicious child, hid the dragon in an outhouse and fed it on milk, keeping it at all times away from her parents. It grew and lost all interest in milk, favouring blood and meat. It started with hens, ducks and geese, but as it grew it graduated to sheep and then to cows. And then to people. In this respect the English dragon seems nastier than its Welsh counterpart. Indeed all Herefordshire 'other' creatures were nasty; if you saw a fairy, it would ask you with which eye you had seen it and then poke it with a bulrush.

Maud, however, was never harmed, maintaining always that it was only bad because people were bad to it. When full-grown it was large, though quite how large depends on the writer. It was at least the size of a large dog, but could have been twelve feet long. Ultimately the villagers wanted it disposed of and, as we have seen with the last Radnorshire dragon, there was a general shortage of knights in armour. Eventually a condemned man called Garson was offered freedom in exchange for killing it. He hid in a cider barrel with the bung-hole removed and shot the dragon with an arrow as it passed him. The barrel was not only to provide cover, but to protect him from the dragon's fiery breath. Sadly, this was not entirely successful because the dragon's final breath either set fire to the barrel or filled it with poisonous fumes. Garson died. As a memorial to the dragon and to Garson a twelve-foot dragon was painted on the church wall. More prosaically, the dragon on the wall was probably a *wyvern*, emblem of St Guthlac's Priory, which owned the Manor of Mordiford. Interestingly, there was a version of the story in which the dragon was converted to peace and sat on the church wall to protect the church, and another that it got tired of the constant battling with the English and went west to sit on a flag. The dragon is no longer on the church wall, though representations of it can be seen in Hereford Museum.

Inside the church, notice the monument to Mary Vaughan who died in 1635. She is shown kneeling in prayer and the inscription notes that she 'Died at her prayers in the forme as you see her portraiture.'

Although Mordiford sits on the Lugg, it is also on the Pentaloe brook, an amiable little stream running in from the east. On 27 May 1811 between 5 p.m. and 9 p.m. there was a violent storm, with lightning, torrential rain and wind. Within those hours the brook had become 180 feet wide and twenty feet deep. It washed away several houses and killed three adults and a child. It was said that it was a 'temporary ebullition.' Such is the way with water.

Beyond Mordiford a modern bridge spans the Wye supporting the B4399 that runs on the south side of the river. Near here in 1920 the largest ever Wye salmon was found, dead. It was 59½ inches long, 33½ inches around, quite a bit bigger than Doreen Davey's fish from the Cowpond near Whitney.

The Wye-follower on the B4399 has passed close to Rotherwas Chapel, a building of various ages up to the sixteenth century, with a curious Victorian spire. It is in the care of the DoE and is worth visiting for the hammerbeam roof alone, even if it is a difficult place to find, the signs being a little inadequate, and the chapel very strangely sited, set among warehouses.

The road skirts Dinedor Hill and village to reach Holme Lacy. The largest house in the county is here. It was built for the Scudamores but is now a hospital. The Scudamores have a special place in the history of the county. As a family their fortune was based on material acquired from monastic houses during the Dissolution, but it was a later member, Sir John Scudamore, who brought great fame to his family and county. Sir John was a soldier who became Ambassador to France in the mid-seventeenth century. From France he brought the forerunner of Hereford cattle and the red-streak pippin, a good cider apple. Cider was a well-known country drink, with references going back to the Romans (who preferred perry) but following the introduction of the better apples it became a county speciality, to such an extent that Hereford produced a *Cider Bible* in which the words now translated as 'strong drink' were translated as 'cider'! Within the county the farm labourer seems to have existed on it, requiring three quarts per day in winter, four quarts in summer and six quarts at harvest. It seems astonishing that they could stay upright long enough to work. With the coming of the EEC and the 'need' to standardize everything, all cider will soon taste the same, whichever litre you sample. But in the county it is still possible to sample brews from different apples and blends. Perhaps try Hagloe Crab, Fox Whelp and Huffcap, but best of all Red-Streak.

The cattle have been called 'the finest and most beautiful of all horned cattle' and it is certainly a pretty breed with characteristic white faces. Indeed to see one of the accredited herds in the countryside when it is at its greenest is to see Herefordshire and England at its best.

The church at Holme Lacy is noteworthy for being, almost literally, miles away from the village. It is, not surprisingly, full of Scudamore monuments and has a fine external monument to one member of the family. This stands, a bronze warrior of full size with a patina afforded by age and birds, to the rear of the church. The church itself is finely situated, the river curving away across the meadows, and has a very fine vicarage beside it. At the vicarage about 200 years ago a giant pear tree split in a high wind, the drooping branch tip-rooting to form a growing arch. The vicar tried the same idea with other branches and created a single-tree arched orchard. In 1796 the tree yielded a staggering fifteen hogsheads, that is 1,500 gallons, of perry. Back on the northern, now eastern, bank of the Wye, the main road passes beside some fine woodland on its way to Fownhope.

Fownhope has one of the finest churches in the valley, a real gem of a building offering a truly English view of a country church from any angle. It is also a large church, one of the largest in the county, and has been referred to as the Little Cathedral. Inside, it has a twelfth-century Norman typanum that is widely held to be the finest in England and draws visitors from all over the world. Less brilliant but of interest is an ancient chest carved out of a single oak tree. Outside, on the main road, are the village stocks and whipping post, which have survived the 200-year period since they became illegal as a punishment. Near them is a milestone dating from the coaching age when distances, apparently, needed to be known very exactly. Hereford, we learn, is 6½ miles and 56 yards away. Which bit of Hereford?

A recently re-printed booklet on the village and its past is available in the church and contains much of interest on the village as it was earlier in the century. It also contains some fine stories offering a glimpse of the country-dwellers' thoughts on townies. One concerns two members of the Ordnance Survey who trampled a garden and offered their official passes to the farmer's

Below Fownhope

wife whose garden it was. When they stopped trampling and moved into an adjacent field, she turned loose the bull, suggesting to them, as they fled before it, that they show it their government papers. Another story, in similar vein, concerns a Londoner who held forth in the inn on reincarnation, intent on educating the peasants. When asked by an old local if he really believed he had been on earth before, the philosopher replied that of course he had, to which he received the withering suggestion that he must have been middling foolish the last time then.

To the north-east of Fownhope is Marcle Hill and the Wonder. The Wonder was that in 1575 the hill 'rose as it were from sleep and for three days moved on its vast body with a horrible noise driving everything before it to a higher ground'. It was said that sheep-folds, hedges, trees and Kyneston Chapel were carried away as the hill 'walked'. The event was long held to be mythical, but in 1825 the chapel bell was ploughed up. Investigations then showed that about twenty acres of land had slid, the rock and soil moving over a clay base. Some of the studies were made by the Woolhope Naturalists Club, named from the village, or more exactly the area around it, between Fownhope and the hill, and one of the county's foremost amateur clubs. The club studies the country's flora, fauna and geology. One late-nineteenth-century member of the club, Alfred Watkins, has attained lasting fame. He deserves to be remembered on two counts, firstly as an early photographer and inventor of photographic equipment, including the bee meter, an exposure meter; and secondly, and more appealingly at this time, as 'discoverer' (or re-discoverer) of ley lines. In 1925 he published *The Old Straight Track*, a book which maintained that Britain was criss-crossed with ancient trackways that were invariably straight and linked distant features, a notch in a mountain ridge, a distinct peak. These trackways, once established, would have contemporary features built beside them, initially *cromlechs*, later churches. The idea for his theory reputedly came when he was in the hills above Bredwardine, and much of the work was carried out in Herefordshire and Radnorshire. One such ley lies at our feet, an (original) Watkins ley linking the churches of Woolhope, Fownhope, Little Dewchurch and Much Birch, the latter two on the far side of the Wye. With the current enthusiasm for earth magic there has been an upsurge of interest in ley lines, not all of it helpful, and the visitor to the Wye Valley who has a copy of Watkins's book will be very well placed to make up his own mind.

Immediately south of Fownhope the minor road (and the Wye) crosses another ley line – one of the problems with the theory is that there are so many. Did ancient man really spend a lot of time traversing the country with two sticks in his hand? This new ley links Capler Camp with Sollers Hope church. The camp is an Iron Age hillfort, with a legend that it contains the graves of soldiers, and so is a natural for the theory. What is distinctly true is that the woodland on the side

Foy

of the hill is excellent. It is the start of a long narrow finger of woodland curving with the river and extending down towards King's Caple.

Sadly, this wood is not accessible to the private visitor, but it does add a dimension to a drive and adds considerably to the scenic beauty of a canoe trip which has passed through mainly water-meadow country for its last meandering miles.

The road leaves the wood near Brockhampton-by-Ross, which has a church that should not be missed. It is an amalgam of many skills, indeed was intended to be just that, and was built by W.R. Lethaby for Alice Foster as a memorial to her parents. It was constructed in 1901-2 and is quite striking with its pyramidal and squat towers and angular gables and doorways. Most surprisingly, except when you remember it is an Arts and Crafts church, it is thatched. Inside, the carpenter, woodcarver, stained-glass-window designer and embroiderer were given their head and have produced a series of very fine works. Nikolaus Pevsner said of the church that it is 'one of the most convincing and most impressive churches of its date in any county. Lethaby gave the church a medieval character without in any way imitating the past.' Who dares argue with such an authority?

Beyond Brockhampton the visitor can swing westward with the river to King's Caple, where a bridge links with Hoarwithy on the western bank. The road to King's Caple passes Fawley Court, a fine mansion. Another fine mansion was that of the Kings of King's Caple, but this is no longer extant.

Those who have travelled the western bank from Holme Lacy to Hoarwithy have had good views across the river, but little that compares with Brockhampton thatched church. There are, however, fascinating links with our earlier journey, as at Ballingham, whose church is dedicated to St Dubricius, already mentioned at Moccas, who was also known as the Evangelist of Archenfield. Archenfield was the name given to the land occupied by an enclave of Welsh to the east of Offa's Dyke. The Wye represented a boundary to the area as far as Monmouth. The name is strange, with many possible derivations: Ergyng or Ereinwg, Welsh for pear orchard; Yrging, Saxon for field; the Romans called it Ariconium, the Normans Arcenefield. Within the area the Welsh had laws of their own, some from their Welsh ancestors, including *gavelkind*, the division of a father's land between his sons. They also had a curious law relating to murder. If an Archenfield Welshman killed a vassel of a Saxon king or *thegn*, he paid a heavy monetary fine, but if he killed another Welshman, then relatives of the dead man met and plundered the killer and his kinsmen, burning their houses and looting until noon of the following day, when the body of the slain was buried. One third of the loot was passed to the King. In exchange for maintenance of these laws and their separate identity the men of Archenfield fought against the

103

River bank at Foy
horseshoe bend

Welsh proper, forming, by custom, the vanguard of advancing armies and the rearguard of returning armies.

Hoarwithy is elegantly named from its grey willows and is well known for the campanile on the church, under which the visitor has to walk to reach the main building. The village, or land near it, was also the setting for a famous river court case early in the century, when landholders of the Wye bank, known as brinkers, were taken to court by the Earl of Chesterfield for fishing in his river. The 'peasants' won the case in 1907, lost the appeal in 1908 and lost again, by one vote, in the House of Lords in 1911. Between Hoarwithy and Ross the river makes an astonishing horseshoe, not only swinging eastward, but running north as well. At the start of the bend at Sellack there was a ford where a descendant of John Kyrle, the Man of Ross, drowned. He had survived three long wars and many battles, only to discover that the Wye was not concerned with a man's courage or luck.

In keeping with the traditions of Archenfield the church here has a unique, for England, dedication to St Tysilio.

The visitor who reaches deep into the horseshoe will find Foy, with a surprising pedestrian suspension bridge that offers very good views of the river but which has been termed 'hideous'. The bridge was originally built in 1876 but was reconstructed only fifty years ago.

The visitor to Foy has to return on the same road, if he has driven, and to make his way to Wilton bridge and Ross, which will be dealt with below. If instead of taking the horseshoe on its inner side the Wye-follower goes on the outside bend he reaches How Caple. One of the miracles officially accredited to St Thomas of Hereford for his canonization occurred here in 1300. Nicholas Fisher, a local boy, fell from his father's boat moored on the river and was drowned. He lay in the water until his father returned and found him. He was lifted out and placed on his bed to be measured for a candle wick, the family being determined to light a candle to St Thomas with a wick the length of the boy. Within a few hours of the decision Nicholas had recovered, a fact confirmed by many villagers who walked to Hereford to attest the miracle.

Beyond How Caple is one of the most delightful sections of river on the Herefordshire plain. For a long sweeping bend of the river the bank can be easily and safely reached. It is a delightful spot. Our bank is tree-shaded, the grass long and soft and speckled with tall, wild flowers. The opposite bank is open, with country views. At the right time a duck may be seen teaching her ducklings to feed among the waterside vegetation, offering encouragement with quiet quacking. It is a very surprising spot, and one that should be savoured at length. Below Ross the valley becomes grander, more majestic, a return to the bolder scenery of Wales, and this is the last place to feel the calmer, meandering river with its flat banks and green water-meadows.

A49

Wilton
Bridge

Ross-on-Wye

203m

Chase
Wood

A40

Walford

A4137

Goodrich
Castle

Kerne Bridge

Goodrich

Welsh
Bicknor

Whitchurch

Huntsham
Bridge

Lydbrook

B4164

Great Doward

King
Arthur's
Cave

Symonds
Yat

English
Bicknor

Little Doward

Seven Sisters
Rocks

Coldwell
Rocks

B4228

Far
Hearkening
Rock

Biblins

The
Slaughter

B4432

A466

Duxton

Suck
Stone

Near Hearkening
Rock

Monmouth

FOREST
OF
DEAN

Kymin

Buck
Stone

A4136

River
Monnow

↑N   Lower Wye Valley Walk
and Offa's Dyke Footpath

B4231

Penallt

Redbrook

Offa's Dyke
Path

Wye
Valley
Walk

Those wishing to follow
the Walks should obtain
O.S. Sheet 162

Scale : Approx. 1 inch to 1 mile

Whitebrook

The Vale (from Ross-on-Wye to the Bristol Channel)

Ross-on-Wye

Those who have followed the Wye down will first see Ross from the main road (A40) as it crosses the river. The bridge offers one of the finest views of the town. Indeed, when the river is calm and the reflection of the town in it is bold, this is as good a view of a town across water as will be obtained anywhere. The shape of the town, set on its pyramidal hill with the church spire surmounting all, lends itself to the scene. Sadly, the possibility of imminent death on the A40, with its attendant noise and fumes, is a considerable distraction. From a road-safety point of view it is as well that the majority of high-speed motorists do not take a long look at Ross, but they do miss an elegant picture as they hurtle past.

A more sedate pace of life exists on Wilton Bridge, a good sixteenth-century construction, though reinforced considerably in this century. It carries an intriguing sun-dial, added in the eighteenth century with an inscription that reads:

> Esteem thy precious time
> which pass so swift away,
> Prepare thee for eternity
> And do not make delay.

This ancient pastime of producing gloom-ridden verses pointing out the mortality of man always seems to me (because I am modern and less religious?) very curious. The sentiments in the first lines of this verse are universally appropriate, however.

From Wilton Bridge the ruins of Wilton Castle tucked away among trees and undergrowth across the river are further signs of the impermanence of man and his structures. The castle was more of a fortified house than a true castle and belonged originally to the Gray family. One of the family personified its character. Fighting for his king in Scotland he 'receaved a greate wounde in the mouth with

a pyke, sutche as clave one of his teethe, strake hym thowroghe the tongue and three fyngers deep into the rouff of his mouthe: yet notwithstondyng hee poursued owte the chase . . .' Under later owners the castle suffered as the third arm of the eternal triangle, being once burnt out by an irate lord when the lady of the house chose another man, and once obtained by another lord when he married another lady. In the latter case it is not clear whether the castle or the lady was the by-product of the real deal and whether the deal was worthwhile. The castle was finally destroyed in the Civil War, having played a good part for the Cavaliers against the Parliamentarians. The last commander was felt by the locals, ardent Royalists, to be insufficiently enthusiastic for the King's cause and so they burnt it themselves. Not surprisingly, the luke-warm follower of the King became a red-hot Cromwellian overnight, but the castle was gone, 'more of spleen and malice than souldier-like designe'.

The river at Wilton Bridge was once used by men in coracles in pursuit of the salmon, and a Wilton man achieved fame for his exploits in one of these small crafts. The craft is a very ancient one, as indeed is the name. The Latin *carsula*, a little basket, could be the source, but the Irish called it a carragh. The local name was never really coracle, but truckle or coble. It was a very light boat, being easily carried on the back, originally made from horse-hide drawn over a wooden frame. Later, canvas was used. The boat drew very little water, making it ideal for a river with frequent shallows, but was very unstable and required enormous skill. A strong salmon was known to drag a coracle for several miles before tiring, and all that time the boat could be upset. Luke Hughes, the local man, gained fame for paddling his coracle to Lundy Island and back, a feat he achieved in two weeks of glorious weather nearly 300 years ago. It was a marvellous achievement and he was feted on his return. Two things should be noted, however: firstly, Hughes was in touch with a boat at all times on his journey, so rescue was at hand; and secondly, he was picked up by a warship at Bristol, the crew of which was so impressed that a very long and very hard party ensued. One source suggests that this occurred on the way out, not on the way back, and may have been the real terminal point of the journey . . .

Beyond Wilton Bridge is Ross-on-Wye. It is difficult to talk about the town, read of it or walk around it without coming face-to-face with the 'Man of Ross', John Kyrle. Perhaps it is advisable to deal with him first so as to set the scene. John Kyrle lived between 1637 and 1724, mostly, for the later part of his life, in Ross. He was born in Dymock, the son of a reasonably wealthy and well-known family, and was left, by his father's death, as a man of limited, but independent, means. His income was £500 per annum, but as he was a bachelor of frugal needs this left him with considerable money to finance his pet schemes. He appears to have been a lonely man, living alone with his house-keeper, Mrs

Bubb, and his one pleasure was entertaining people to dinner once a week. His only other vice, if vice is the right word, was a curious ring he had made. It was a ruby set in gold, and when the stone was touched, it opened, a hissing snake's head emerging from beneath it. With his income Kyrle gave the town a great number of things, a water supply being the most obviously laudable. River water was pumped to a fountain and then piped to public taps. He also restored the causeway to Wilton Bridge, erected seats, rebuilt the church spire and constructed, or helped to construct, several public buildings. On the Market House, opposite his own house (suitably marked as such) in the town square Kyrle placed a bust of Charles II and a curious logo. This is in the form of a C and F intertwined with a heart and was short-hand for Kyrle's monarchist loyalties – Faithful to Charles in Heart. When he died, at the great age of eighty-seven, Kyrle was said to have been penniless, having literally run out of money on the day of his death. If this is true, it is quite extraordinary and confirms the author's opinion that parents should leave their children only that which is vital to their (the parents) continued life – house, some money etc. – and a bill for the funeral.

Kyrle's benefactions were impressive, but unlikely to have achieved any great and lasting fame – indeed within a few years of his death he was largely forgotten, with no real memorial. However, Alexander Pope was at Holme Lacy and in need of a man of excellent virtue for his *Moral Essays*. Pope wanted to distinguish the man of real and solid worth, not just showy expense, and so strike a blow to the pride of 'greater' men, and eulogised Kyrle as the Man of Ross in a long, and largely indifferent, poem. Today it is difficult to escape from the Man of Ross, as opposed to John Kyrle, and this has been true for some years; the old coach from Ross to London (in only fourteen hours!) was named Man of Ross. So, it would appear, is everything else. It comes as a surprise that the take-away pizza house is not. But that is cynical. Kyrle was obviously an honest, if slightly unimaginative, man of good local standing. His gift of the spire on St Mary's church almost makes the town, for it is this, as we have seen, that helps produce the excellent view of the town from the Wye. The church also forms part of a curious Kyrle story. Kyrle planted elm trees along the side of the church in 1684 and one of these produced suckers inside the church near his own pew. The suckers produced fine trees that grew up in the windows, receiving light through them, until they died when the parent tree was felled in 1878. Now virginia creepers grow from a soil box as a memorial of the trees and of Kyrle. Sadly, the other elms died of Dutch elm disease and had to be felled. He also donated the peel of bells, throwing his favourite silver tankard into the molten bell metal. In the churchyard there is a less happy memorial, a plague cross commemorating the deaths, in 1637, of 315 townsfolk who are buried in a communal pit to the west of the cross.

The Church at Ross

Ross-on-Wye market

The vicar at the time, John Price, was a man of great courage, who visited the sick and buried the dead with some semblance of a Christian burial service. Eventually he rallied the town's dwindling population and they processed around the Market Square singing the Litany. At once, it seems, the plague abated. Opposite the cross are the Rudhall almshouses, a fine late-sixteenth-century building. John Kyrle helped provide food for those who lived here.

Ross was a village in Saxon times and is the reputed site of the death of Edmund Ironside in 1016. At that time the English kingdom was divided between Edmund and Canute, and a slave of Edmund decided to kill his master for the great reward Canute would give him. To that end he placed a sharp stick in the King's latrines (!) and held the candle away as Edmund used them (!!). The King was heavily impaled, as we can well imagine, though it is something I would rather imagine than witness. The dreadful deed reputedly took place at the King's 'villa' at Minsterworth in Gloucestershire, so why he should have been brought to Ross to die is a mystery. Was he on the way to a holy shrine for a cure? The servant rushed to Canute with news of his great deed. Canute hanged him from the highest oak tree that could be found. This is, perhaps, punishment fitting crime, and Ross has a history of such things. In 1305 sixteen men who felled trees in the Bishop of Hereford's wood were fined and ordered to walk around the town on one Sunday and one Market Day, the leaders on two of each, dressed only in their shirts. Since Ross is a high and windy place the villagers were delighted and felt badly let down when the Sunday turned out to be St Mary Magdalene's Day (the patron saint of penitents), a hot still day in July.

It is such things that raise the spirits of a community. When Sir George Cornewall Lewis, whose stone image we have seen in Hereford, lost an election locally in the mid-nineteenth century, the townsfolk, true Liberals, were incensed. A well-oiled mob held the victorious Tory candidate by his feet from the upstairs window of a local inn and he was made to shout 'Cornewall Lewis for ever' as an alternative to being dropped on his head. Later still Market Day was enlivened by an inept escape artist who habitually chained himself to a lamp-post and writhed and struggled for hours until he begged for help. And there was the rat-catcher whose wife was ill, mainly as a result of poor nutrition. The doctor suggested to the man that he should sell his dog and buy a pig (i.e. for fattening). The man thought for a long time and then suggested to the doctor that it was a poor idea – a pig could never catch rats like a dog!

Below Ross the river has carved a valley with high, wooded sides that has been called the finest piece of river scenery in Europe, and as a result the valley has

113

always attracted the visitor. The story is often told of two travellers of the nineteenth century who were arguing about the best drives in Britain and who agreed to write down their own preferred drive for the on-lookers to judge the finest. One wrote Ross to Monmouth, the other Monmouth to Ross, and the judges declined to decide the better. Ross has always attracted visitors intent on travelling south to Monmouth and beyond. Today we can follow the Lower Wye Valley Walk, a complement to that we followed from Rhayader, or canoe the shady waters of the river.

But originally the tourist was here for the Wye Tour. In one sense the Tour started in 1750, when Dr Egerton, later Bishop of Durham but then Rector of Ross, and his wife travelled down the river to Tintern. While that was a forerunner, the Tour proper only really existed from 1760, when James Evans, a basket-maker of Ross, first hired boats for the purpose. The Rev. William Gilpin, whom we have met before in the Introduction, with his, to us, strange 1782 book *Observations on the River Wye*, advertised the tour as a must for any followers of the cult of the picturesque, and his book was followed by others, most particularly Charles Heath's brilliant 1799 book *The excursion down the Wye from Ross to Monmouth*, which ran to many editions, each of which increased trade a little more. The Tour was made in a boat rowed by from two to six men depending on the size of the party. The Tourers were well catered for, an awning keeping most of the rain off them, a central table being provided for writing and sketching, which also frequently groaned under the weight of food and drink provided for the healthy appetites of the occupants. The trip, which was usually only downstream from Ross, cost 1½ guineas if Monmouth was the terminal town, this being a day trip, and 3 guineas if the tourists went to Chepstow, Monmouth then being used for an overnight stop. Some boats even plied from Hereford, the extra stage from there to Ross being another 1½ guineas. As usual, the early tourist made much of the objective dangers of the tour: 'if there be ladies in the party', then an experienced boatman was an absolute requirement, etc.

The Tour received a boost in the early nineteenth century, when the Napoleonic Wars put an end to European travel. A more stable Europe meant decline for the trade, but there were still people interested in the mid-nineteenth century. In 1865 Prince Arthur, aged only thirteen years, helped to row from Ross to Chepstow in non-stop pouring rain.

Today at Ross the Wye-follower will find no pleasure boat for hire to take him to Monmouth or beyond. He could paddle his own canoe, and will be amply rewarded if he does; try to hitch a ride on a passing raft during the annual charity raft race down the public section of the river; or follow the Lower Wye Valley Walk. We shall look more closely at the latter, mention the former and omit the middle option as being unlikely. The thirty-four-mile Lower Wye

Goodrich Castle

Valley Walk is, in contrast to the Upper Walk, very well signed and there is available a set of plastic cards with full-colour sections of the relevant Ordnance Survey map, the route marked in. From Goodrich Castle southward the route can be followed on the 1:25000 O.S. Outdoor Leisure Map, Wye Valley and the Forest of Dean.

Ironically, in view of the name, the walk starts by deserting the river, moving east from Ross, then south to climb Chase Hill through its excellent woodland and over the ditch and rampart remains of the Iron Age hillfort that surmounts it. The walk then drops down through pleasant country to Kerne Bridge, where there is one of the best views on the whole river, of the ruins of Goodrich Castle over the water. North of here, at Walford, Hill Court is a large and excellent late-seventeenth-century mansion. The name derives from Welsh ford, a ford also used by the Romans; as if to prove the Roman connection, a horde of 18,000 coins was dug up in the nineteenth century, the horde being contained in three fourth-century urns.

Kerne Bridge was not built until 1828 and was then a toll bridge, the old toll house still standing at one end. Before the bridge there was a ferry here, used by Wye Tourers to cross the river to visit the ivy-clad ruins of the castle. This is curious, for it implies that the Tour boat landed on the east bank so that tourists could catch another boat to take them, presumably at a price, to the west bank. Now I am sure that the Tour boatmen had lots of good reasons why they could not land on the west bank, but the chief one, probably unstated, was that it was their relatives and friends that ran the Goodrich Ferry. In 1388 the Earl of Derby, later to be Henry IV, arrived at this spot on his way from Ross to Monmouth, the last leg of a journey from Windsor, by a bit of a strange route, to see his wife. Then, as 400 years later, there was a ferry, and the Earl asked the boatman if there was news from Monmouth. 'There is, my Lord,' the man replied, 'you have a son' – the future Henry V having been born at Monmouth. The Earl was overjoyed and asked the boatman if there was anything he wanted to repay the great news he had passed on. The boatman asked for, and was given, ownership of the ferry and the right to the crossing. The ferry stayed in the family for generations. The castle that stands above Kerne Bridge was one of the high spots of the Wye Tour and is still an excellent site. Then it was ivy-clad and romantic, now it is cleaned up, less romantic maybe, but more accessible, and better able to stand the rigours of time. The village and castle take their name from one of three people, Goda, sister of King Edward the Confessor; Godric, Abbot of Winchcombe, near Cheltenham, who owned the land; or Godric Mappestone, the owner at the time of the Domesday Book, usually credited with having built the first castle. The earliest surviving work is from the twelfth century, the magnificent square keep, there being work from each century from then to the sixteenth. The whole, as we now see it, is a superb and elegant example of the castle builder's art, and a living history lesson to the younger Wye-follower. Here there have been, and traces are still visible, drawbridge, portcullis and moat, the tower buttresses to withstand battering and, best of all, the dungeons, still dark and evil. The site is wonderfully evocative of castle life, the views to the river are magnificent and, best of all, there is no car park to intrude on the scenery and the quiet, since it is set a few hundred yards back at a picnic site. But castle sites are not chosen for aesthetic reasons; this was a war engine, guarding the river crossing. As if to prove the point, one owner, Sir John Talbot, was a veteran of forty battles who died, sword in hand, at his forty-first at the age of eighty. As a war engine, though, 'this castle was a very good pile', and proved as much in the Civil War, when it was held for the Royalists by Sir Henry Lingen until all the rest of Herefordshire had fallen. In his efforts to maintain the castle, Sir Henry was helped by Thomas Swift, Vicar of Goodrich and grandfather of Dean Swift. Thomas and the local blacksmith made 'cats', three pointed iron 'things' that they sat in the ford under water to cripple the advancing Parliamentarian cavalry. Horses were hurt and the cavalry retreated in confusion, leaving time to clear the castle of its treasure before the final assault came. On 5 June 1646 Col. Birch of the local Parliamentarian army asked for 'some battering pieces for Gutheridge'. The Commons decreed that '80 barrels of powder be forthwith provided for the service against Gotherich Castle and Ragland Castle, out of the store at Oxford', which shows that they wanted Goodrich taken, even if they also could not spell its name. Birch was also granted 'two mortar pieces and other equippage . . . and the great Iron Culverin'. This latter may have been Roaring Meg, a mighty cannon, though we also read that Birch 'cast a mortar piece here, which carries a shell of 200 lbs weight'. Roaring Meg, still preserved at Hereford, was a fearsome weapon, as can be imagined, firing a ball weighing close on two hundredweight. By 6 July 1646 it was said that 'Colonel Birch goes on well against Gutheridge castle, and is like to carry it suddenly.' The defenders were not done yet, however, and came out one morning catching the Roundheads unawares, killing eight men and capturing the mortars. Unable to carry them or break them, or just unaware of what it was they had captured, the Royalists poured poison into the muzzles so as to kill the guns! This seems ludicrously funny to us now, but how sad, how pathetic, it really was. On 31 July Goodrich surrendered, Sir Henry Lingen and forty-three men being taken prisoner. Only Pendennis Castle held out longer.

Thomas Swift had left Goodrich earlier and taken his entire family fortune, 300 gold coins, sewn into his waistcoat, to the King at Raglan. The King was delighted. Swift's family (he had fourteen children) were ejected from the vicarage by the victorious Roundheads, starving and destitute. On a happier note, it was

Whitchurch (between
Goodrich and
Symonds Yat)

at Goodrich that Wordsworth is said to have met the little girl who inspired 'We are seven', written in 1793. One later writer spoke to a man who could remember this story from his grandmother. She wasn't the little girl, the writer asked incredulously. No, the local replied; actually I think she was the only girl in the village who wasn't!

Before we leave Goodrich, consider one last fact. The castle had, as was usual, an earth floor. It was widely stated that the earth for Goodrich was imported from Ireland since it was known that toads did not like Irish soil!

Below the castle, at the western end of Kerne Bridge, is a farm/craft shop, parts of which are the remains of Flanesford Priory, an Augustinian house of the mid-fourteenth century. The long barn contains the old refectory. If the visitor to Goodrich has arrived by car and now drives back to the main A40 at Old Forge, he will rejoin the river after about one mile. If the visitor is in a canoe he will reach Old Forge after seven miles of steady paddling; such is the meandering of the river. One old writer called these large curves the 'sinuosities' of the river.

But we are following the Wye Walk, and the next section of it is a superb piece of walking, on the inside of the long horseshoe bend of the river. The far bank represents the western boundary of the Forest of Dean at this point, that realm of ancient laws and beautiful woodland that the Wye-follower should visit soon. As the tightest part of the bend is reached, the Walk passes Courtfield, a fine house on the site of the home of the Vaughans, a well-established local Catholic family. The house still bears an ancient sign of the family, also used on their signet rings, of a child and snake, a reminder of the encounter a young Vaughan had with an adder on the house lawn. The snake was found twined around the child by his nurse, who fetched a saucer of bread and milk which she placed near the pair. The snake left the child for the saucer and was promptly killed. It is a good story but I find it hard to believe that adders eat bread and milk. Another interesting story concerning a young family member tells of a time when a father Vaughan was walking with his son on the estate. The son had been married a long time but had no children, a fact which vexed his father. During the walk they reached a gate and the father challenged the son to vault it. This he tried, and failed. The older Vaughan vaulted it with ease. 'As I have cleared the gate for you,' he said, 'so I must also provide you with an heir.' And so, at seventy-five years old, he married, fathering another son and three daughters.

It is stated that it was to Courtfield that the young future Henry V was brought to be nursed by the Countess of Salisbury. An effigy in Welsh Bicknor Church, a little further down the walk, is said to be of the Countess. But, some experts maintain that if Henry V was here at all, then his nurse was Lady Montacute, and that the effigy at the church is not possibly the Countess because it is 100 years too old, or too new – a veritable confusion of expertise.

Welsh Bicknor

Before Welsh Bicknor is reached, Lydbrook is passed on the opposite bank. This was reckoned, in the 1860s, to be comparable with Sheffield as a centre for industry, with factory chimneys, furnaces and boats constantly plying the waters of the Wye. There is still industry there, but it no longer makes an impact on the river or valley scene.

Welsh Bicknor is a tiny village, beautifully set, and here the Wye Walk crosses the river by a footbridge that is a disused railway bridge, to visit the English side of the river. The village on this bank is English Bicknor, the difference between the two names signalling that there the river divided England, not from Wales as you might expect, but from Archenfield. The English village has the remains of a Norman castle, its church standing in the castle courtyard, and a court with Tudor remains. The Wye Walk now stays on the English bank to take the next horseshoe bend on its outer side, passing Coldwell Rocks. The rocks themselves are good, a foretaste of the rocky scenery in store as we travel downstream. The name is an ancient one and derives from a local source of frigid water that had disappeared or, at least, could not be traced by the Wye Tourers of the 1800s. The Tourers ate a meal at this shady spot, and an unfortunate result of this is commemorated by the memorial on the far bank. In 1806 the Warre family were among Tourers who stopped here, and after the meal John Whitehead Warre unwisely went swimming in the river. He had cramp and sank like a stone. One John Smith dived in to attempt a rescue, but the youth was a lifeless deadweight and Smith had to leave him in order to save himself. When retrieved, young John was dead. His family raised the stone which has been the subject of abuse ever since. One early traveller noted that 'the epitaph is tedious' but was appalled that 'some wretch has lately mutilated the monument'. He did not note the real mistake, however, that despite the notice given that life-saving apparatus and instructions are lodged at Coldwell Church, anyone in trouble should not hold his breath and await formal rescue. There is no Coldwell Church. There has never been one.

Beyond Coldwell Rocks the Wye Tourers left the boat to visit the Symonds Yat rocks to admire the views, which really are worth seeing, descending to the river on the western side of the rocks. This walk was about half a mile, their boat travelling about four miles in another horseshoe bend around Huntsham. The Wye Walk takes a compromise route, going north of the rocks, but still crossing the low-lying land encircled by the long bend. This section of river completes the long meanders that the river needs to reach a point one mile from Goodrich. The canoeist could be forgiven for wringing his hands or carrying his boat if it were not for the scenery he passes.

Symonds Yat is a marvellous spot, with something for everybody – quiet woodland walks, rapids for canoeists, rocks for climbers, riverside pubs for the

Symonds Yat

more cautious traveller. It has good geology, bird-life, flora. It usually has too many people. Today the casual visiter does not have to walk up from the river; he can drive to the forest car park at the top and amble pleasantly across to the rocks. One Tourer noted that the climb to the rock, 'though a work of some toil, will reward the curious observer'. It was maintained at that time that the rock was at least 2,000 feet above the river. The problem of having such an excellent survey of Britain is that a glance at the map shows this to be an error of about 1,500 feet.

The name is strange, and not as readily explained as some would have us believe. The standard explanation is that Symonds is from Robert Symonds, a seventeenth-century High Sheriff of Herefordshire, with Yat from the Saxon *gate*, a track. Others have offered differing solutions, with Yat meaning rock, an unlikely explanation, and Symonds from Seamans, in reference to a Danish invasion route. This latter is interesting, which is not to say correct, as there are many legends of battles close by, at the Slaughter and on Doward Hill.

A walk to the Yat rock or towards the isolated pinnacle of limestone near the cliffs will be worthwhile. At the right time of the year, or even of week or of day, when the area is quiet, this is a delightful spot, with something to hold the interest at every turn. For the river walker, the ferry near the riverside inn on the western bank is great fun. For a nominal fee the walker can change banks, sitting it out while the ferryman drags the boat across the water hand over hand along an overhead cable.

The canoeist too is well catered for, the Symonds Yat rapids offering a couple of hundred yards of interesting fast water. The run is straight, and straightforward enough, but has the boat slapping at the water a few times to make life exciting.

The limestone rock that outcrops near and at Symonds Yat, also outcrops on the far bank at the somewhat unimaginatively called Severn Sisters rocks. These are in fact quite interesting as they were undercut by the river when it ran much higher than today. That is not to say it was deeper, just that it had not cut such a deep channel. Above the rocks is King Arthur's Cave, excavated in 1870 by dynamite to reveal the (shattered) bones of mammoth, cave bear, woolly rhinoceros and hyaena. The name is meaningless, a quick survey of Welsh caves suggesting that the only caves not associated with Arthur are those associated with a Llywelyn or Owain Glyndwr. The cave is in the side of Doward Hill, with a fine Iron Age hillfort surmounting it. This is glorious limestone country with the usual wide variety of flora. Over 700 species of flora and a further 300 mosses and liverworts have been identified in this area. The hill itself is associated with Caratacus, the Welsh tribal leader who fought against the Roman invaders for many years. He is reputed to have camped here with his army before the battle against the Romans under Ostarius Scapula which gave the opposite band its

The Ferry at
Symonds Yat

Yew trees, the Forest
of Dean

name, the Slaughter. Caratacus was forced ever northward by the Romans and eventually betrayed into their hands. So impressed were they with his conduct of the campaign and by his dignity in captivity that he was not executed but escorted to Rome, where he lived as an honoured guest.

During excavations on the hill arrow heads were discovered, as were a collection of bones. They were in a natural cave that a sheep entered, followed by a curious observer. The collection started a local murder story, but the bones were obviously very old. The bones in one set were twice the size of the others, implying that they were from a man between ten and twelve feet tall. A legend had maintained that some who had escaped with Vortigern from a battle at Amesbury had made their way here, although it is a strange place to choose to die. One local doctor who examined the bones suggested they were of a large dog, a story contradicted by the finder who suddenly remembered a body that fell away to dust when touched. It was probably just another twelve-foot Welsh giant.

Until 1920 there was, inside the fort, a hexagonal tower about fifty feet high and made of iron. It was built by the eccentric owner of nearby Wyastone Leys so that he could see the Severn. Sadly the Kymin near Monmouth is very high and he ran out of enthusiasm.

From the hill the view across the river to the Forest of Dean is stunning. Within the forest here are several interesting outcrops of rock. There are the Far and Near Hearkening Rocks, reputedly named from their use by gamekeepers listening for poachers. There is the Suckstone, a 4,000-ton monolith and, most famous of all, the Buckstone. This was a *logan*, or rocking stone, so perfectly balanced that not only a person but a strong gust of wind could set it gently rocking. On 10 June 1885 it was overturned by a few vandals. The outcry was considerable, those responsible being 'excursionists', 'idle, mischievious and selfish'. At a cost of £500 the stone was restored to its position, but it no longer rocks. The name is said to derive from the fact that deer used it for shade, or because a deer jumped on it to escape hunters, although this is unlikely as it offers no real escape. Clearly at one time the stone was held in awe. Though now known to be natural, a detached mass of Old Red Conglomerate, it was thought to be Druidic in origin, a sacrifice stone, and was supposed, when rocking, to ring the fate of a battle.

The canoeist, after he has passed the rapids at Symonds Yat, has some of the most pleasant miles of gentle river that he has passed since Glasbury, with tree-lined banks and calm waters. The footbridge at Biblins is a landmark, but this area would not now be recognized by the Wye Tourers. When they came here this was New Weir, and an iron forge belched out black smoke and fiery cinders, the forge hammer thundering away amid piles of ore and coal. It is difficult to imagine now.

Near Martin's Pool

Here also is Martin's Pool, believed to be the deepest on the river, perhaps measuring sixty feet. In it lies a silver cup dropped by a Wye Tourer and never recovered, or so the story goes. Beyond, the river turns sharp left, and then swings gently right to approach Monmouth, its church spire beckoning. The last mile is measured out for the Monmouth Rowing Club and their regattas, and the canoeist can try a sprint of a few hundred yards if the gentle waters upstream have made him idle. On this stretch the visitor, be he walking or paddling, as the Wye Walk follows the river consistently, also re-enters Wales, the county of Gwent.

The first village is Dixton, with a church so close to the water that it is little surprise to learn that it has been flooded often. Indeed, there is a plate inside giving the depth of water in the church in recent floodings. In 1852 the churchwardens had to pay the sexton 2s. extra when they required him to wade out through several feet of water to toll the bell for the death of the Duke of Wellington.

Monmouth

An American visitor to Britain once wrote that 'he who visits England without seeing Monmouth and the River Wye does not know what beauty there is in Old England'. Now anyone who votes Plaid Cymru might be forgiven for choking on the reference to Monmouth, England, but the sentiments are true enough. Monmouth is a delightful spot, situated at the junction of the Monnow and the Wye, the former river giving the town its name, from a shortened form of Monnowmouth. In Welsh it was Abermynwy, but is now Trefynwy, the town on the Monnow.

A marcher castle was built here, of course, mid-way between Chepstow and Clifford, and there was a Benedictine priory very early. This was possible because the semi-Welshness of Archenfield meant less trouble, and because it was a Breton family that held the land. Since the links between Brittany and Wales are strong, this was an advantage. The priory was in a fairly serious state by the time of the Dissolution, everything that was not screwed down having been sold off by the last-but-one prior, one Richard Evesham, for his own gain. Evesham seems to have been the kind of house master that gave Henry VIII all the excuses he needed to dissolve the houses, quite easily living up (down?) to the description of 'detestable, shameful and unclean.'

During the Civil War the Roundheads took Monmouth and ordered that the castle be slighted (that is, the walls were partially destroyed), though it was in a poor state anyway, leaking and with the wind able to blow through the walls. The town seems to have been little troubled by the War, a fact that would probably not have held true if Cromwell had been assassinated here in 1646. A Royalist hothead called Evans was making ready to shoot him when some townsfolk, sensing a bloody aftermath to such a deed, prevented the killing. Once Cromwell had departed Evans was freed.

The Roundheads were appalled by the road system in Monmouthshire, which seems to have been worse than that further north. The army commander maintained that every lane was a pass to be disputed. Later it was noted that on one occasion a judge could not reach the town because the road, which was fifteen feet below ground level, was impassable, and a little later still, when Valentine Morris of Piercefield (which we shall pass) was questioned in the House of Commons for proposing a County Turnpike Act, he maintained that there were no roads in the county at all, the inhabitants travelling in ditches. Despite the difficulties of the roads, however, the town was captured, the castle slighted. A later writer wondered 'that the transmutations of time are often ludicrous – [the castle] was formerly the palace of a king, the birthplace of a mighty prince: it is now converted to a yard for fattening ducklings'.

Monmouth Bridge

The Royal reference is to the birth in the town of the prince who became Henry V. A statue of the king stands in an alcove on Shire Hall looking out on Agincourt (what else?) Square. It is not a good work, making the king look, as one traveller had it, like a hypochondriac inspecting his thermometer. A much better statue is also in the Square, one of C.S. Rolls (co-founder of Rolls Royce) who lived nearby. He is shown looking at a model of an early 'plane, a reminder of his untimely death in a flying accident in 1910. Staying with the well-known who are associated with the town, mention should be made of Geoffrey of Monmouth, the early-twelfth-century ecclesiastic who wrote the *History of the Kings of Britain*, a very readable book full of wild inaccuracies and good legends. It is likely that Geoffrey was brought up in the vicinity, perhaps nearer to Caerleon than the town itself. Davy Gam, whom we have met before, the knight of Agincourt and model for Fluellen, was also a local. He lived at Llantillo and it was said that if all his children held hands they could reach from his house to the church. It sounds reasonable enough until you find that it is a very long way. And lastly John Frost, a name that many can be forgiven for greeting with: 'Who?' Frost was leader in Monmouthshire of the Chartists, that strange, usually ill-understood movement, who wanted government to yield on the six points of its People's Charter. These included universal suffrage and secret ballots, things that today we take for granted but which, in the 1830s, caused the hearts of those in power to stop. By November 1839 Frost was convinced that there was to be a general uprising of Chartists throughout Britain and organized a march of the men of South Wales on Newport. He had hoped for 50,000, but in torrential rain far fewer, perhaps only 5,000, turned up, mainly unarmed or armed with pitchforks and clubs. They marched into Newport and at the Westgate Hotel met the mayor, who had about thirty soldiers with him. There were shouts on both sides, a shot, from whose gun is not clear, a volley from the soldiers and the rain-sodden, dispirited men fled. Twenty-two men lay dead or dying. Frost was captured and was brought to Monmouth for trial with Zephaniah Williams and William James, his deputies. On 16 January 1840 the three were sentenced to death by hanging, their bodies to be quartered. Virtually the full medieval sentence.

The men shared a cell in Monmouth Jail, listening to the carpenters outside constructing the gallows on which they were to die. But sense, or at least the desire to have no martyrs, prevailed and at midnight a fortnight later the three were handcuffed and taken to a boat at Chepstow *en route* to Van Diemen's Land. Fifteen years later they were pardoned and Frost returned. He died in 1877 aged ninety-three.

As much as for people, the town is famous for caps. The trade was excellent, for in the early 1500s cap wearing was compulsory on Sundays and saint days and each class of society had its own style. There are instances of people being fined for wearing caps 'beyond their station in life.' The trade was good for everybody, because the cap material was wool and the British economy was based on it. Not for nothing does the Lord Chancellor sit on the Woolsack. The caps of Monmouth were famous; even Shakespeare has Fluellen comment on them in *Henry V*, including the probably authentic touch that the Welsh wore leeks in their Monmouth caps. The centre for the industry was actually Overmonnow, but as it was largely cottage-based the town also benefited. It also benefited from the Wye, which was straightforwardly navigable at this point, facilitating considerable trade, including ship-building and repairs. The trades based on the river did not prevent occasional depressions in circumstances of the town, and Monmouth like other towns had its workhouse. Here, in order to raise extra duty to pay for the poor, the town council came up with a tax on swearing, levied at 1*s.* per word. I imagine that in the boat-yards the idea was both profitable and unpopular. Neither was the river always popular; sometimes the townsfolk found that it flowed 'copiously, against their will into their dwelling houses.' Despite that and the two rivers that border the town, one nineteenth-century visitor noted, to his utter astonishment, that the townswomen bought soft water at 6*d.* the half-hogshead. River water, it seems, was not good enough for washing, though at the same time it was felt that to be immersed in the Wye waters as they rose was a cure for bites by a rabid dog.

No visit to the town should pass without a walk around it, for although its river frontage is very poor, with no advantage having been taken of the town's greatest asset, the array of fine, mainly Georgian, buildings is very worthwhile. The first worthwhile building to see is the gate on the Monnow Bridge. This positioning of a gate is unique to Monmouth. Elsewhere be sure to see the Beaufort Arms, a Regency coaching inn in Agincourt Square standing beside the equally impressive Georgian Shire Hall. Also worth visiting is St Mary's Church, a fine building with an elegant 200-foot spire that was such a dominant feature of the view southward as the Wye-follower approached the town.

And finally the Free School, endowed by William Jones in the late sixteenth century. Jones was born in Newland around 1545 and was forced to leave the area when a young man because he was unable to pay a bill of ten groats. He fled to London, where he made a fortune from Welsh cotton, returning to Wales in order to put the money to good use. The story is told that he dressed as a beggar and returned to Newland, where he was disgusted by the treatment he received. He then came to Monmouth, where he was kindly received, and so it was here that he built the first school. The foundation stone of the new school laid in 1864 lies over a bottle containing one of each of the coins in circulation at the time, and a vellum scroll with words as inscribed on the stone. The inscription starts:

Near Monmouth

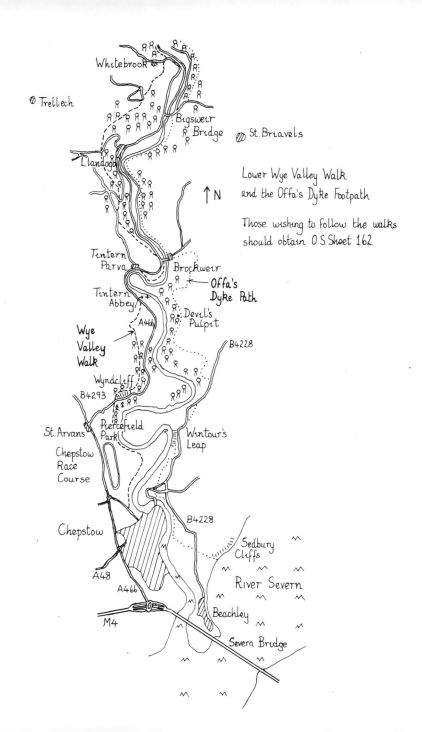

Whitebrook

⊘ Trellech

Bigsweir
Bridge

⊘ St.Briavels

Llandogo

Lower Wye Valley Walk
and the Offa's Dyke Footpath

↑N

Those wishing to follow the walks
should obtain O.S. Sheet 162

Tintern
Parva

Brockweir

← Offa's
Dyke Path

Tintern
Abbey

A466

Devil's
Pulpit

Wye
Valley
Walk

B4228

Wyndcliff

B4293

St. Arvans

Piercefield
Park

Wintour's
Leap

Chepstow
Race
Course

B4228

Chepstow

Sedbury
Cliffs

A48

River Severn

A466

Beachley

M4

Severn Bridge

'This Free Grammar School Founded with the Almshouses adjoining by William Jones Esq. AD 1614.'

From Monmouth the walker is spoilt for choice, for in addition to the Lower Wye Walk, which we shall follow, there is also the Offa's Dyke Long-Distance Footpath, which completes its 165-mile journey from Prestatyn to the Severn by following the Wye to Chepstow. This latter route will also be mentioned here, as it follows an elegant line mainly on the Valley ridge tops, occasionally visiting an interesting spot missed by the Wye Walk. One such site can be visited immediately the route leaves Monmouth. The Wye Walk stays with the river, crossing to the eastern bank at the town's Wye bridge and continuing down the bank to Redbrook. The Offa's Dyke Path climbs eastward from the same bridge, leaving the river to visit the Kymin, an 800-foot hill almost due east of Monmouth. On the Kymin are two buildings from another age. The first is the round tower or Pavilion, built in 1793 by the Kymin Club, a very exclusive group of local gentlemen centred on Monmouth, for their weekly dinners. To that purpose it contained a kitchen and banqueting hall and, later, a bowling green and stables. So far, so good, but the lay-out of the windows was to suit a purpose that today sounds a little odd. It was decided that each window would be specifically aligned 'to give foreground with objects immediately before the eye, from left to right. To extend the sight as far as the foot of the hills, terminations carrying the eye on, as before. To increase the sight to the utmost boundary of the horizon – adopting the same manner in conducting the view from left to right.' There was, then, for each of the windows a discourse on the foreground, horizon etc. with a list of the intended sights. The view from window 1 was terminated by Dundry Tower near Bristol, while window 3 had the Blorenge and Sugar Loaf near Abergavenny. Now I have to confess that the passage quoted above, like the passages from Gilpin on the 'picturesque' Wye, leave me wondering. I can understand composition in art, but am less able to comprehend an attempt to enforce strict laws of composition on to unaltered (as opposed to Capability Brown) landscapes. The view from the Kymin in any direction is good, in some directions superb. I suppose the better ones are better composed, but I would rather look than analyse. However, during a crucial period of construction, the sun set and the moon rose at precisely the same time. This was seen as auspicious. I bow to greater natural forces.

The Naval Temple beside the Pavilion was raised by the same group, assisted this time by public subscription, on the second anniversary of the Battle of the Nile, to commemorate the battle and its victor and other historic battles and admirals. A contemporary writer wrote that the opening of the Temple, on 24 June 1801, was 'one of the THREE days of PUBLIC TRIUMPH at Monmouth'. The first was 19 August 1799, when colours were presented to the newly formed

135

Redbrook

corps of Volunteer Infantry; the second was the opening of the Kymin Naval Temple; the third, and most important, was '19 August 1802 when THE HERO OF THE NILE came for a public dinner in his honour and to see the Naval Temple.' The hero in question was, of course, Nelson, but you need to know that before reading the account, because only this expression, in capitals, is used in the article. Nelson arrived by boat, the last two miles of the journey between banks crowded with cheering people. The band played 'See the Conquering Hero Comes'. The crowd roared for their 'Great and Darling Son of the Ocean'. Nelson was impressed: 'Had I arrived', he said, 'at any of the great sea-ports of the Kingdom, I should not have been much surprised at this token of attachment from my Jolly Jack Tars, but to be known at such a little gut of a river as the Wye fills me with astonishment.' Clearly the great man had little truck with false modesty, nor was he a great diplomat. 'Little gut of a river'? How did the crowd take that? – they applauded, saying his deeds made his name known and respected in every part of the civilized world. When Nelson visited the Temple and looked at the painting of the Battle of the Nile, with opera glasses, he made no comment and showed no emotion.

Beyond Kymin the Offa's Dyke Path drops gently down to the river at Redbrook. The Wye Walk also visits Redbrook (the paths touch at that village), having stayed at the water's edge all the way from the Monmouth Wye bridge. Before Redbrook is reached, Penallt can just be seen across the river, a village famous for its pudding-stone, or breccia, millstones, some of which are still visible in the river into which they rolled. They were made on the hill and rolled down for sale. Here Richard Potter, chairman of the Great Western Railway Company, lived, one of whose daughters, Beatrice, married Sidney Webb. Penallt was then visited by the Fabians, George Bernard Shaw writing *Arms and the Man* here.

Redbrook is split into two villages, Upper and Lower, and was once a notable industrial area, visited by the now long-gone Wye Valley Railway. There was copper making here and a rolling mill. It is now all gone. To see this part of the valley, say from Redbrook to Tintern, now, the great cleft of the Wye gorge, its sides tree-lined with occasional houses, the water crystal clear, it is difficult to imagine that it was once an intense industrial site, and difficult to be sorry that the factories are gone. The Wye Valley represents perhaps the finest unspoilt river valley of its length in Britain. It is ironic that in this lower reach with its apparently primary woodland cover, the landscape we see has been reclaimed by nature.

Beyond Redbrook the Offa's Dyke Path returns to the valley top to follow an actual section of the great Dyke itself. It then drops off the ridge to Bigsweir Bridge. A little over a mile south-east of the bridge is St Briavel's, more a Dean

Forest village than of the Wye, but worth visiting for all that. It has a curious ceremony held annually on Whitsunday in the churchyard, when bread and cheese is distributed to the congregation and a collection is taken. The ceremony has taken place outside, and in a civilized manner, since 1857. Prior to that, the bread and cheese were thrown inside the church, with the congregation scrambling on the floor for them. By 1857, however, the church was filled by hooligans on the day and the whole ceremony became slap-stick, but without comedy or much dignity. The ceremony is ancient, possibly a pagan spring-triumphing-over-winter rite. More likely, especially since the congregation each paid 1 *d*. before the distribution, was that it was to preserve an ancient right, perhaps to use land as common, or to take wood. Such custom-preserving rituals are not uncommon, and indeed it appears that St Briavels at one time had two. The other one concerned the wife of the governor who rode naked around the village once a year, *à la* Godiva. Now why this should be and whether the village watched is lost in the mists of time, but it is known that King John came one year and liked the ceremony so much that he ordered that all the young girls of the village should do the same for his benefit. After that the original ceremony seems to have fallen into disrepute.

The Wye Walk does not visit Bigsweir Bridge, as it leaves the western bank of the river – it changed from east to west bank by the old Redbrook Bridge – at Whitebrook to explore the beautiful wooded ridge above Llandogo. Whitebrook is another old industrial village now largely returned to the natural state. The inhabitants here have always been in touch with nature. On May Day they rose with the sun to gather dew, which they used to wash their faces since it guaranteed a beautiful skin. They then gathered hawthorn twigs in full blossom to decorate their May-pole. It is as English a scene as you could wish to see in any village, in Wales.

After Whitebrook the Wye Walk, among the trees of Cuckoo Wood, is half-way between Trellach and Llandogo. The former is not a Wye village but is an interesting spot. In fact it is three interesting spots. First there is St Anne's or the Virtuous Well, a chalybeate spring used by pilgrims and water-takers. For the latter it would 'expel ennui from the most desponding hypochondriac'. It was also used by the fairies who danced around it on Midsummer's Eve and then drank from it on Midsummer's Day, using as cups the harebells that grew nearby.

Secondly there is Terret Tump, a large mound said to be a burial ground for the dead of Earl Harold Godwinson's army after a battle with the British near here. To substantiate this there is a local field, Bloody Field, that will grow only gorse no matter how many times it is ploughed, because it has been soaked with blood.

Brockweir

Lastly there are Harold's Stones, a line of three standing stones said to have been erected to commemorate Harold's victory. Another legend links them with Jack of Kent, a local giant or warlock who may have thrown them here from Skirrid mountain near Abergavenny, or who competed with the Devil in stone throwing. Jack threw first, then the Devil threw, further, and finally Jack threw, furthest of all. It seems an unfair competition if the Devil had only one throw, but that is the way with some of these tales.

Llandogo, a true Wye village, climbing gracefully up the western side of the valley, white houses peering out of the tree cover, is another relic of the industrial past. The river becomes tidal at Bigsweir Bridge, but it is here that the signs are first obvious. This is a shame, since Llandogo is such a pretty village and the mud banks do little to enhance its appearance. The village has a Sloop Inn, a reminder of the time when such boats could sail comfortably up to this point in the river. Beyond, a flatter-bottomed boat was needed. The local name for the boats was trow, and that name is commemorated at the other end of the journey on the Welsh Back in Bristol, where an old sailing-boat inn still stands, the Llandoger Trow. There is no mistaking the nautical nature of that old inn – it was the model for The Spyglass in *Treasure Island*.

The church here is dedicated to the sixth-century saint, St Oudoceus. He was offered land here by a knight, as much as was encircled in a day by a hunted deer. St Oudoceus wanted to build a monastery, but the dogs were not good, or the deer too clever, and all he got was space for a *llan*. That and his name have given the village its name. The river here has been fished for elvers, the young of eels, as well as salmon. In fact one man, many years ago, caught nine hundred-weight of them in one night. What did he do with so many?

The avid river-follower could, in fact, have carried on along the western bank of the Wye when the Wye Walk left it, to arrive at Bigsweir Bridge. From there the Offa's Dyke Path has alternative routes, one going east and then south parallel to, but removed from, the river, the other going along the eastern bank to Brockweir and its bridge. There it rejoins the Wye Walk, which has traversed Bargam Wood with its viewing points for magnificent views to the valley and then dropped down to Brockweir. Brockweir is another pretty river village with a history of ship building and fitting, suffering from its closeness to Tintern. The canoeist sees its bridge as the landmark before the horseshoe bend to Tintern and the best landmark of all, the Abbey set high on the bank against the woods.

Offas Dyke by the
Devil's Pulpit

Tintern

The Offa's Dyke Path does not visit Tintern Abbey, climbing again onto the eastern ridge and following it through the woodland to avoid the long meander around Lancaut, heading directly for Wintour's Leap. It does, however, pass the Devil's Pulpit, an isolated rock from which the Devil harangued the monks as they built the great abbey, and catches, at Ban-y-gor Rocks, a first glimpse of the Severn. The Wye Walk sticks to the western bank, first visiting Tintern Parva, Little Tintern. This tiny village with its own church had a separate identity when the area was famous for its wire-works. Now that has gone and it is the Abbey alone that attracts the money, the village is a quieter, more subdued place standing aloof, away from the hubbub just down the street.

Tintern Abbey was the highspot of the Wye Tour, and no wonder. The site is exquisite, the remains sufficiently intact for a real appreciation of the monastery, its size and lay-out. The whole has been called the most beautiful ruin in Britain. When seen in the misty morning of a clear day with the leaves of the trees behind a summer green, or autumn gold; when viewed by the light of a full moon, a hooting owl adding to the atmosphere, it is easy to see why this has been said. In the past, when the ruins were ivy-clad, not gaunt and bare (though, it must be added, less likely to collapse as a result), it must have been even more romantic. Not so to all, you will be surprised to hear. When Gilpin came he noted: 'it has been an elegant Gothick pile', but added:

> 'though the parts are beautiful, the whole is ill-shaped. No ruins of tower are left, which might give form, and contrast to the walls, and buttresses, and other inferior parts. Instead of this, a number of gable ends hurt the eye with their regularity; and disgust it by the vulgarity of their shape. A mallet judiciously used (but who durst use it?) might be of service in fracturing some of them; particularly those of the cross isles, which are not only disagreeable in themselves, but confound the perspective.'

It does indeed take all sorts.

Prior to the abbey there is no authenticated history of Tintern, although a legend has it that its Welsh name, Din Teyrn, is from Dinas Teyrn, the fortress of Teyrn or Theodorick, King of Morgannwg who was killed here in a battle with the Saxons around 600 AD. The abbey itself was founded by Walter de Clare, Lord of Chepstow, as a penance. It is probable that his sin was killing, and it may even have been his wife that he killed. He sought help from a priest who sent him on a crusade. He showed great bravery in repeated attempts to get himself killed, but returned unscathed to endow the abbey as a final penance. The foundation was in the twelfth century, for Cistercian monks, but the abbey as

Devil's Pulpit

Wye at Tintern

it is dates largely from the thirteenth century, when it was rebuilt by Roger Bigod, the Earl of Norfolk. The Earl obtained his curious surname from confrontations with his King. The King on one occasion shouted that Roger must go, or stay and be hanged. Roger replied, 'By God, Sir, I will neither go nor be hanged' and was Roger Bigod thereafter. There is, perhaps, evidence in the charter of grants to the abbey that Roger drew up that he was also doing penance:

> 'Be it known to your community (of the church of St Mary de Tynterne) that I, in the sight of God, and for the health of my soul, and the souls of my ancestors, and heirs, have confirmed to you divers lands, and possessions . . .'

The monastic way of life seems strange to us today, and it is difficult to understand how so many abbeys and priories could have existed and how so many monks could have been supported by an agriculturally based peasantry. But flourish it did, although a decline had set in before Dissolution brought about an end to the life-style. At Dissolution, Tintern, like monasteries elsewhere, was stripped bare of its treasure and its roofing and then plundered for its stone. The abbey did constitute a fairly handy quarry. In the mid-eighteenth century it was systematically cleared out. The workmen discovered a number of bodies in an orchard, lying not in coffins but under plain stone slabs. When unearthed they were intact, but fell to dust soon after. The workmen were discussing the discovery in the main abbey over their dinner when there was a 'fearful darksome gloom . . . clouds dissolved in tears at the sacreligious intrusion . . . forked lightning angry flashed against the gothic pillars', and the ladies of the village maintained that the founding lords themselves had walked as a judgement on the disturbing of the dead.

It may have been that this tidying of the site was carried out in expectation of the Wye Tourers and the money that could be earned from them. When Gilpin arrived, an early Tourer as we have seen, the locals do not appear to have been in economic distress. He notes that 'among other things in this scene of desolation arrived an early Tourer as we have seen, the locals do not appear to have been in economic distress. He notes that 'among other things in this scene of desolation the poverty and wretchedness of the inhabitants were remarkable. They occupy little huts, raised among the ruins of the monastery, and seem to have no employment, but begging . . . As we left the abbey, we found the whole hamlet at the gate, either openly soliciting alms, or covertly, under the pretence of carrying us to some part of the ruins.' Gilpin and his party engaged one old woman, who offered to show them the monk's library:

> 'She could scarce crawl, shuffling along her palsied limbs, and meagre, contracted body, by the help of two sticks.'

From Wintour's Leap

But it was not the library she wanted to show the Tourers, 'it was her own mansion . . . I never saw so loathsome a human dwelling.' It was a cave, the walls running with water, the floor mud. She had no furniture or utensils, though she did have a bed covered with rags. Gilpin and friends 'were rather surprised, that the wretched inhabitant was still alive; then that she had only lost the use of her limbs.'

It is an extraordinary picture of poverty and degradation in the Britain of two centuries ago. What would the Cistercian monks have made of this scene? And what would they have made of the scene today with its bustling tourists?

Let us leave the site with the monks in mind. Gilpin maintained that theirs was a life 'devoted to indolence', a good Protestant attitude, but one unlikely to have been true. The lowly monk was much more likely to have been honest and sincere, devoted to his life of austerity and the canonical round. The abbey was for him. It is he, and the master mason, who should be remembered when viewing the church windows, the finest Gothic windows in Britain, or when walking the cloisters.

The monks' life was not all tranquillity in the valley, for it was they who brought iron-making here. The great forests offered unlimited charcoal for the smelting; only when coking coal was discovered did the importance of the area decline in favour of South Wales. Brass was first made in Britain at Tintern, as a plaque tells us, and the metal bridge that crosses the water once carried a tramway to the wire-works, a history that a plate on it proudly records. Here too ran the Wye Valley Railway. The old station is being re-opened as an exhibition centre, and out of the valley to the west an old furnace, charcoal-fired and water-powered, is being conserved.

Beyond Tintern the canoeist must proceed with caution; the tidal effects on the river are increasingly severe and he who arrives at Chepstow at the wrong time can find himself a mud-wall away from where he would like to be or, far worse, on his way to the treacherous waters below the Severn Bridge.

It is best to walk, the Wye Walk leaving the river to climb up through woodland to the Wyndcliff by a fairly direct route. The river has no desire for a direct route. Sensing that it will soon be just another anonymous band of water in the Channel, it twists left and right to stay within its beautiful wooded valley. From the Wyndcliff the view is excellent, as good as at any point on our journey. Below, the river makes its long bend around Lancaut and the tighter bend at Wintour's Leap. The cliffs of the Leap stand out white among the woods and the elegant sweep of the Severn Bridge draws the eye towards the Cotswolds.

The top of the Wyndcliff is 700 foot above the river, though not all of that height is climbed by the 365 steps laid out in 1828 by staff of the Duke of Beaufort who owned much land around here, including Tintern Abbey. The local Preservation Society has done valuable work on repairing the steps, reducing the number to around 300, but who would bother to count? One Victorian writer was glad of the trees which obscure the drop – without them, he said, he would have been dizzy; and the staircase section of the walk – it really is a staircase up the side of a steep cliff section – could still make those who have no taste for heights swallow hard. The visitor who baulks at the thought must glance quizzically at the climbers on the cleaner, steeper faces. For the visitor who climbs, try Questor; it's not the hardest route, but in my view it's the best. But even if you are not a climber, the Wyndcliff will delight with its abundance of limestone flora.

After the Wyndcliff, the Wye Walk descends to traverse Piercefield Park, now the home of Chepstow Racecourse, but once the home of Valentine Morris who laid out the western bank of the Wye as a walk with ten viewpoints that embodied the Picturesque, that crock of gold we have sought before. Valentine Morris was a likeable spendthrift. He succeeded to a fortune when his father died, including property in Antigua, and determined to create at Piercefield a paradise on earth, a temple to the picturesque. He employed William Knowles of Chepstow, a landscape architect, to assist him, and together they laid out a series of walks between ten viewpoints. Each viewpoint was fancifully named – the Chinese Seat, the Druid's Temple – and equipped. Thus the Grotto, a cave made from solid rock, was filled with copper and iron cinders. At each viewpoint there were seats so that the visitor could take in the view. The intention was that the full view would not appear until you were seated; a black mark against Morris was the fact that many believed that the views were too easily seen *before* the seat was reached, and that there was an absence of cascades. I must confess to my old misgivings about composing nature. In this case it is backed up by the knowledge that Piercefield, when complete, was valued at £50,000, and that in the late eighteenth century. At the same time Morris bought a slave for his Antiguan plantations, and called him Piercefield. He paid £10 for the man.

Morris was an extravagant man who entertained lavishly and, ultimately, added gambling to his list of vices. Eventually in 1770, when giant ants attacked his Antiguan plantation and they made no profit for the year, he went bankrupt and had to sell the park and to head for Antigua. When he departed from Chepstow the church bell was muffled and rung and a sorrowing crowd lined the streets. Morris was so touched that he cried. He did well in the West Indies and was appointed Lieutenant Governor of St Vincent. At his own expense he prepared the islands for defence against the French but lost everything when the French invaded. The pain of this second bankruptcy drove his wife insane and Morris was imprisoned for debt in England despite the fact that the government owed him more than the total of his debts. It was a sad case of bureaucratic bungling, but it was never resolved and Morris died in poverty.

The Wye Walk does not visit all of Morris's viewpoints, but the general effects can be seen as the horseshoe bend at Lancaut curves away towards Wintour's Leap. Near here a local proverb was enacted, for it was said that the man born to hang will not drown. Thomas Moxley was on his way to Chepstow one night 'somewhat disguised with liquor' (what a wonderful phrase!) when he fell off a cliff and down towards the river. He broke a leg and was badly injured but survived drowning as the tide was going down, leaving the bushes in which he landed high and dry. Concussed and unable to move, Moxley lay waiting for the next tide to engulf him, but his groans were heard by fishermen riding the tide, and they rescued him. He recovered well and two years later stole a horse — for which he was hanged at Monmouth Jail.

By following the Wye Walk the visitor avoids traversing the top of the cliffs of Wintour's Leap, although he does see them from across the water. Here too is a playground for the rock climber, though some of the routes are very serious, long and with rock that needs delicate handling. The cliff is named for Sir John Wintour, a Royalist sympathizer in the Civil War. Wintour fortified his own mansion at Lydney, though he was away when a Roundhead army called. He need not have worried, for his wife defended the house so strongly that the Roundheads retreated, weary. Sir John was anxious that the cliffs near Beachley should be fortified, the Severn at that point being easily crossed by barge, as the later Aust-Beachley ferry showed. He was about this business when his group was surprised by a contingent of Roundheads under Colonel Massey. The Royalists were heavily defeated, some, including Wintour, scrambling down the Sedbury cliffs to the safety of boats. This escape is likely to have given rise to the legend of Wintour's Leap, with Sir John leaping down the shallow cliffs on horseback. A later action, near Lancaut, also saw Wintour involved in a last-minute retreat and it is probable that it was this event that gave rise to the naming of the cliffs, with the horseback leap being transferred here in popular imagination. It is, after all, unlikely that Sir John leapt down these cliffs, in one go or several, and survived.

Beyond the cliffs the Offa's Dyke Path visits Chepstow on its way to its end point at Sedbury Cliffs, and our walk also visits the town, which marks its end.

Chepstow Castle

Chepstow

The Wye Walk follows a wooded trail near the river until the very doorstep of Chepstow is reached. The woodland here was famed as a poaching ground and produced some great characters who brought colour to the local scene. One famous local walked stiff-legged at all times to try to disguise the times when he did it because he had to, a gun barrel being pushed down each trouser leg. Ultimately he was caught for pheasant shooting. His defence was straightforward: 'Indeed your honour I never shot no pheasants at all. The only bird I shot was a rabbit, and I knocked that down with a stick.' Case dismissed surely!

The woods and river could be hazardous though, especially if the traveller was a little unsteady. One unfortunate started shouting 'Man lost!' when he became hopelessly entangled and panic-stricken. An owl answered 'Whoo-whoo' and he yelled back that it was the clockmaker from Chepstow.

The Welsh had a settlement of some form here, calling it Ystraigyl, the bend, and this name was taken up by the Normans who called their first castle Striguil. The name Chepstow is Saxon, market town, the word *cheap* for market having survived often as Chipping and even at Cheapside in London, so there must have been a Saxon settlement as well. The currently approved Welsh form is Cas Gwent from Castell Gwent.

The first castle was built by William Fitzosbern, one of the Conqueror's chief advisers, in 1067, though it was much extended and restored later. The town walls, including the Portwall and the superb town gate, were added two centuries later. The gate is not itself original, having been much renovated over many centuries and almost entirely rebuilt in the early 1500s. William's son Roger, who succeeded to the lordship in 1075, was less well favoured by the King when he led a revolt against him. Perhaps anxious that the famous family should be for him and not against him, William sent Roger a set of robes as a peace offering. Roger burnt them. When he heard of this, the King noted that Roger was a proud man, 'but he shall never come out of prison as long as I live'. Nor did he. The castle passed to the de Clare family, one of whom, Gilbert, was surnamed Strongbow. Our river has passed through cider country, but this lord was not pre-named for that, but for his enormous strength and ability to draw a long-bow. He had six fingers (that is five and a thumb) on his right hand and very long arms, being able to touch his knees with open palms without bending. Despite this, which must have given him a strange appearance, he was 'a very parfait gentil knight'.

At later stages the castle was a prison for Edward II before he was taken to Berkeley and murdered, and for the father-in-law of Edward IV before he was taken to Kenilworth for execution. So much death, but then that is why it was built at all.

The bridge at
Chepstow

In the second Civil War, of 1648, there was more blood and death when the castle was captured and held for the Royalists by Sir Nicholas Kemeys. The threat this posed was enough to bring Cromwell to the scene and the castle was badly damaged by cannon fire. Sir Nicholas had left boats as a means of escape, tied up at the foot of the castle wall, but a Parliamentary soldier swam the river and cut them free to drift away. After that the castle wall was breached and many Royalists ran out to surrender. Terms were offered and refused, the breach stormed, and many men, Kemeys included, were killed. A plaque marks the spot of his death. Today the invading horde is of tourists and the castle that once rang to the screams of the dying is filled with the laughter of children. It is a better noise. Those used to the more compact Edwardian 'circle of stone' castles of North Wales will find the plan here a little unusual, but the views of the river are excellent, and the stonework impressive.

Ironically, in view of the capture of the castle by Parliament and the killing of Kemeys, the castle was soon in use again as a prison for Sir Henry Marten. Marten had been one of those who signed the death warrant for Charles I, suggesting that the signatories 'should serve His Majesty as the English did his Scottish grandmother, and cut off his head'. Later he refused to agree to Cromwell accepting the crown; at least he was consistent, but he was imprisoned for life after the Restoration! It was widely held that had he been really dangerous he would have been executed, but that he was allowed to rot away here, a despised fanatic. This conflicts with the idea that he was a 'sturdy and intellectual republican', but at this remove it hardly matters. Whatever his intelligence he stayed in Marten's Tower for twenty years. His life was pleasant enough, he was allowed friends and often went out to dinner. These latter trips were not always successful, Marten being totally unrepentant. Once, at dinner at St Pierre, he was asked what he would do if he had his time again. He quickly replied that he would do the same and his stunned host countered that he would never, in that case, come to his table again. And he did not. At seventyeight years of age Marten died; he is buried in the town church under a slab bearing indifferent lines of verse, the main purpose of which was to spell out   HENRY   MARTEN with the first letter of each line. At first Marten lay in the chancel, but a vicar named Chest had him dug up and moved, as he would not suffer a regicide to be buried in such a place. Rev. Chest was obviously an odd man. When he died his son-in-law wrote his epitaph:

Below Chepstow

Here lies at rest, I do protest,
One Chest within another;
The chest of wood was very good;
Who says so of the other?

As if that were not enough of odd epitaphs, the churchyard holds Elizabeth, wife of John Webb, who died in 1758 aged forty-six having 'travailed with 28 children'.

Chepstow has always been a market town, as the Saxon name indicates, and as such has always been relatively prosperous. It was not always wholesome, however: in 1804 the parish accounts note that Thomas King, the town crier, was paid 1s. for 'Crying Piggs not to be suffered about the Streets,' and later the market sold opium and fine healthy leeches openly. To this market prosperity was added the profits of ship building and engineering, the latter still carried on by the local firm of Fairfield Mabey, bridge builders. It is one of their bridges that spans both Wye and Severn. In keeping with engineering being a local forte, the tubular suspension bridge built by Isambard Kingdom Brunel to take the railway over the Wye was itself a major first for the town. The bridge needed underpinning and a new main span a century later, and is not as elegant as the road bridge near the castle, nor as scenically positioned, but it still has its admirers. So too has Chepstow town, and a stroll around its sloping streets is an excellent way of completing the Wye Walk.

Both bridges span the Wye and it is to that we return. The tidal effects at Chepstow have caused some extensive flooding, the river once rising seventy feet in one tide, and once coming up so fast that a woman and girl were drowned in bed. But it is more renowned at this point for being the grave of 'evidence' that Francis Bacon wrote Shakespeare. The supposed evidence was a complete set of manuscripts in Bacon's hand, plus supporting notes telling the story of why he had persuaded an unknown Stratford actor to accept responsibility for them. Their whereabouts had been discovered by Dr Orville Owen of Detroit, who had unravelled clues left by Bacon. Dr Owen arrived in Chepstow in 1909, first searching a cave near the castle, then building a coffer dam in the river to search the bed. The good doctor eventually retreated empty-handed.

After flowing under Brunel's bridge the river swings right, then left past a sewage works, before accepting defeat and flowing its last mile without any bend at all. It passes the modern castle, the Army Apprentices School, and then flows under its last bridge, a mere arm of the Severn road bridge. This is a toll bridge, a final link with the river's Welsh origin, shades of Rebecca at Rhayader. Then the river joins the Severn. Yards apart on Plynlimon at birth, together as they are lost in the sea.

The Wye waters entering the bigger river cause some minor eddies, then they are gone.

The water changes, but the river goes on for ever.

The Severn Estuary,
where the Wye meets
the Severn

Index